D. H. Lawrence in New Mexico

"The Time Is Different There"

ARTHUR J. BACHRACH

Photographs by Charlotte Page

UNIVERSITY OF NEW MEXICO PRESS

∾

ALBUQUERQUE

© 2006 by the University of New Mexico Press
All rights reserved. Published 2006
12 11 10 09 08 07   2 3 4 5 6 7

LIBRARY OF CONGRESS CATALOGING-IN-PUBLICATION DATA

Bachrach, Arthur J.
    D. H. Lawrence in New Mexico : the time is different there /
Arthur J. Bachrach ; photographs by Charlotte Page.
        p. cm.
Includes index.
ISBN-13: 978-0-8263-3496-1 (pbk. : alk. paper)
ISBN-10: 0-8263-3496-2 (pbk. : alk. paper)
    1. Lawrence, D. H. (David Herbert), 1885–1930—Homes and
haunts—New Mexico—Taos.
    2. Lawrence, D. H. (David Herbert), 1885–1930—Friends and
associates.
    3. Authors, English—20th century—Biography.
    4. Taos (N.M.)—Biography. I. Title.
PR6023.A93Z563 2006
823'.912—dc22
                          2006008935

HALF TITLE: Detail from window in Mabel Dodge Luhan's bathroom,
    painted by Lawrence and Brett. Photo courtesy of the author.
FRONTISPIECE: Painted door from Pink House (see pages 41–43).
    Photo courtesy Kevin Cannon and Rena Rosequist.
DESIGN AND COMPOSITION: *Mina Yamashita*

To the memory of a good friend,

a fine storyteller, and a *bon vivant*:

Saki Karavas

∾

And what about the ranch,

the little ranch in New Mexico?

The time is different there . . .

—D. H. Lawrence,
"A Little Moonshine with Lemon" (1926)

Contents

List of Illustrations

Acknowledgments

There have been three key events in my learning about D. H. Lawrence. The first happened when I was at the University of Virginia. Through mutual friends I met Emil Schnellock, a professor of art at Mary Washington College, the University of Virginia's campus in Fredericksburg. Emil introduced me to the works of D. H. Lawrence, as well as those of Henry Miller, of whom he had been a childhood friend. Emil's knowledge of art and literature was profound, and his enthusiasm contagious. It wasn't until recently, when I read Karl Orend's interesting "Afterword" to Fraenkel's *The Otherness of D. H. Lawrence*, that I learned that Emil had been a member of the Parisian "Villa Seurat" group, which had among its members Henry Miller and Anaïs Nin, both devoted Lawrentians. I will always be indebted to Emil Schnellock for his warmth and his mentoring. Karl Orend has been most generous with sharing his broad knowledge.

The second key event was a workshop on Lawrence's

days in Taos held at the Mabel Dodge Luhan House in Taos. The instructor was David Farmer, a Lawrence scholar and an inspired teacher. His overview of Lawrence in Taos rekindled my interest in Lawrence and his work.

The third key event was an international conference held in Taos in 1998 by the D. H. Lawrence Society of North America. I was privileged to act as site director, ably assisted by Debra Holte. This conference, and the international conference in Santa Fe in 2005, afforded me the opportunity and pleasure of working with Earl Ingersoll, Keith Cushman, Hugh Witemeyer, and Virginia Hyde, all of whom have become prized friends. Keith Sagar's presentation at the Santa Fe conference reinforced the fine scholarship for which we have always been indebted. I am grateful to another friend and Lawrence scholar, Nicole Tartera-Velebni, for her stimulating discussions on Lawrence during her frequent visits to Taos.

I am deeply grateful to Nita Murphy of the Southwest Research Center for her invaluable archival skills, and to Pamela Body for her fine editorial help in the preparation of the manuscript. I am also indebted to Barbara Cobb for her excellent final copyediting.

My thanks also to Robert and Linda Attiyeh and their excellent staff at the Mabel Dodge Luhan House for their warm support. They, and Lois Rudnick's writings, have brought new life to Mabel Dodge. To "Bonhomme" Richard W. Godin, my gratitude for sharing his prized collection of Mabel Dodge Luhan documents. ∾

CHAPTER ONE

Lawrence's Early Years

ENGLAND AND EUROPE

D.(avid) H.(erbert) Lawrence was born in Eastwood, England, near Nottingham, on September 11, 1885. His father was a coal miner and his mother a factory worker, although she is often described as a school mistress, emphasizing a difference in class status that actually did not exist. His mother did encourage Lawrence's educational goals. As a young man, he began to write and published his first novel, *The White Peacock*, in 1911. In 1912 he met Frieda Weekley, the wife of a former professor of his at Nottingham University, and ran off with her; she left her husband and three children. They married, in London, after her divorce in 1914.

Lawrence was never a strong person. During World War I, he was rejected by the army and, as he reported it, was humiliated in the examinations they forced on him, an experience he tells vividly in the "Nightmare" chapter of his novel *Kangaroo*. He and Frieda had a difficult time during the war. She was German and an aristocrat, daughter of Baron Friedrich and Baroness Anna von Richthofen; the baron was a cousin of the German war ace "The Red Baron" von Richthofen.

In 1916 the Lawrences were living in Cornwall, on the coast—an especially difficult experience during which they were harassed by the police, suspected of being spies, and eventually, in 1917, ordered to leave. Among other accusations, they were reported to have been singing songs in German.

Frieda recalled the tense situation in a "conversation" on D. H. Lawrence held at UCLA in 1974:

German folk songs, English folk songs. We would sing a lot. And that was so dumb of them. We had about five dollars a week to live on in those days, and so how could we support submarines and sea-spies?[1]

They moved to London. Lawrence's passport was confiscated, and he was unable to leave England until 1919.

In addition to the political harassment, Lawrence suffered from attacks by the literary establishment and censors. In 1915 his novel *The Rainbow* was declared obscene by the authorities and the book was seized and destroyed, almost shattering his literary career. In fact, he was able to sell only one short story in the following three years. The situation was sufficiently difficult to make the Oxford University Press, which was publishing Lawrence's school textbook *Movements in European History*, suggest that he use a pseudonym rather than his real name. Lawrence agreed and selected "Lawrence H. Davidson," a name that remained until the 1925 edition of the book carried his real name.

In 1919 Frieda returned to Germany and Lawrence to Italy, and in 1920 they were reunited in Italy. Again the literary establishment, this time using the journal *John Bull*, attacked Lawrence's work. *John Bull* had attacked *The Rainbow* and now reviled *Women in Love* with a headline that read, "A BOOK THE POLICE SHOULD BAN: Loathsome Study of Sex Depravity—Misleading Youth To Unspeakable Disaster."

The review reached Lawrence in Taormina, Sicily, at

the Villa Vecchia and greatly upset him. He wrote a letter to his friends Earl and Achsah Brewster—an American couple who were living in Ceylon—in which he vented his anger. The Brewsters were studying Pali, an Indian language of a Buddhist sect. Lawrence invoked "a curse, a murrain, a pox on this sniffling, spunkless brood of humanity" who had attacked his work.[2] He asked the Brewsters about possibly going to visit them in Ceylon.

On October 8, 1921, Lawrence had written a rather prophetic letter to his American publisher, Thomas Seltzer:

> I wish I could find a ship that would carry me round the world and land me somewhere in the West—New Mexico or California—and I could have a little house and two goats, somewhere away by myself in the Rocky Mountains.[3]

On November 5, barely a month after his letter to Seltzer, Lawrence received a package from Mabel Dodge Sterne, earnestly inviting him to come to Taos, enclosing some herbs (*desachey* and *osha*) and an Indian necklace for Frieda. (*Desachey* is an "Indian perfume," made from such flowers as alfalfa and thistle; *osha* is a plant in the privet family, the root of which is prized for its medicinal value.) For Lawrence, she sent a copy of Charles Lummis's book on New Mexico, *The Land of Poco Tiempo* (land of "pretty soon"). Lummis, whose book was published in 1896, was the first one to use the term "The Southwest." Lawrence accepted the invitation, and Frieda wrote an eager approval of the plan. But Lawrence hedged, and Frieda wrote Mabel in late January that Lawrence said he wasn't strong enough yet to face America.

CEYLON AND AUSTRALIA

Lawrence decided to go to Ceylon to visit the Brewsters, to whom he wrote, "I will go East, intending ultimately to go West." Lawrence and Frieda arrived in Kandy, Ceylon, on March 13, 1922. He had looked forward to seeing Ceylon, but by the end of March he had had enough of the "silly, dark people," "the nasty faces and yellow robes of the Buddhist monks, the little vulgar dens of the temples." Lawrence's first impression of Mabel's house, when he finally arrived in Taos, was of a cluttered, dim, candlelit home that reminded him of "one of those nasty little temples in India."[4]

His remark found other expression later in a story he wrote called "Things," in which he satirizes Mabel's living room and has a little sport with his friends the Brewsters. The protagonists in "Things" are an American couple who travel around the world studying "Indian thought" and collecting bric-a-brac.

From Ceylon, Lawrence intended to make his way west by way of Australia and the Pacific. He loathed New York and wished to travel to Taos, if indeed he ever did, via the West Coast of the United States.

Six weeks after his arrival in Ceylon, the Lawrences set sail for Australia. During the sea voyage, Lawrence met an Australian named Scott, who told Lawrence about a secret, right-wing army being formed by a group of ex-servicemen in Australia to fight the perceived threat of Communism and take over the government. Scott's motive was to enlist the aid of this internationally known writer. The Australian people were apparently unaware of the existence of this secret movement until years later, but Lawrence presented an accurate view of the movement in his novel *Kangaroo*. He was apparently aware of his possible transgression and betrayal of Scott's confidence by revealing this secret group, as evidenced in his letter to Seltzer that October from Taos, where he was completing the manuscript for *Kangaroo*: "Do you think the Australian Govt [*sic*] or the Diggers might resent anything?"

This episode reveals several important elements of Lawrence's personality. One, he drew upon real persons and real events in his novels. Two, he did not seem to care about what others might consider betrayal by transforming real people—friends and associates—into fictional characters. He offended a good friend, Katherine Mansfield, by using her as a basis for a figure in a novel, and another friend, the British composer Philip Heseltine, sued Secker, Lawrence's publisher in England, for slander because Lawrence had used him as a character in *Women in Love*. Lawrence did this to many of his friends, including Mabel Dodge Sterne (later Luhan), upon whom he drew for Lou Carrington (the central figure in his story "The Woman Who Rode Away"), and Dorothy Brett in "The Princess" and his short story "The Last Laugh."

To be sure, Lawrence also drew upon himself (and

Frieda) as characters in his fiction. In *Women in Love*, which so upset Heseltine, Lawrence used himself as a basis for Birkin, one of a group: "Halliday, Birkin, the whole Bohemian set, they were only half men."

In Australia, Lawrence was, as ever, ambivalent, enjoying the scenery but fearing it was seducing him from his English work ethic—a "lotus-land." On August 10, 1922, Lawrence and Frieda sailed from Australia to Roratonga, where they spent a few days, then to Tahiti. Lawrence, characteristically, found the country beautiful to look at, but felt that the South Sea Islanders were "centuries and centuries behind us in the life struggle."

Lawrence's ambivalence about his frequent travel was summed up in one of his observations: "Travel seems to me a splendid lesson in disillusion." There were great hopes and inevitable disappointment, but often he would later write nostalgically about places he had visited— places he seemingly despised while he was there, but which he would view with a different eye at a later time. Mabel Dodge Luhan, in her *Lorenzo in Taos*, insightfully commented that "Lawrence couldn't live with pleasure in the real moment. He lived afterwards." ∾

CHAPTER TWO

Taos I

September 1922 to March 1923

PATHS TO TAOS

I have adopted Eliot Fay's[1] convention of referring to the three periods the Lawrences spent in Taos as "Taos I . . . II . . . III."

It is often noted that Lawrence's travelogue *Sea and Sardinia* led Mabel to invite Lawrence and Frieda to Taos. In October, 1921, Mabel read the issue of the cosmopolitan literary magazine *The Dial* that contained excerpts from *Sea and Sardinia*, a book that *The Dial*'s editor, Scofield Thayer, had urged Lawrence to write. Mabel's letter of invitation to Taos was dated November 5, 1921, a full month before the book's actual release date of December 12, 1921, so the invitation was apparently based on the bits from the book published, along with some of Lawrence's other writings, in *The Dial*. These bits of writing had convinced Mabel that Lawrence was the writer to do justice to Taos and to her Indians.

Mabel was, in her own way, making a significant impact on the literary world. In her book *Movers and Shakers*, she tells of her "salons" in New York, which many of the most important literary and art figures of the time had attended. Among her circle of friends were the author and critic Max Eastman, artist Carl van Vechten, journalist Walter Lippman, and Communist author John Reed, who wrote *Ten Days that Shook the World*, a book about the Russian Revolution. Her liaison with Reed added a political side to Mabel's intellectual development.[2] Max Eastman was also a Socialist associate of Reed's who influenced Mabel. Eastman later recanted his leftist beliefs in the time of McCarthyism, but John Reed is buried in the Kremlin.

In the January 1920 issue, *The Dial* had published an article by Walter Pach, a friend of Mabel's, on "The Art of the American Indian." In March of that year, *The Dial* presented three watercolors by Native American artists, including the Hopi Fred Kabotie's *Hopi Snake Dance*. All three artists were noted as represented in Mabel's collection of art.

Lawrence's relationship with *The Dial*, despite occasional problems with its editors, was fruitful. From September 1920 to July 1929 (its last issue), *The Dial* published thirty works by Lawrence in twenty-five issues.

THE LAWRENCES ARRIVE

The Lawrences arrived in San Francisco, and on September 4, 1922, Lawrence wrote to Mabel that he and Frieda were at the Palace Hotel with about $20 to their name. Mabel had wired them Pullman tickets for the trip to Lamy, New Mexico (outside Santa Fe), and Lawrence's agent, Robert Mountsier, provided them with travel money. On September 10, Mabel Dodge and her then chauffeur (and lover), the Taos Pueblo Indian Tony Luhan (they married the following year), met the Lawrences at the railroad station in Lamy. There was a certain awkwardness as they dined at the railroad station and then left in Mabel's car, driven by Tony, for Santa Fe. On the way, the car broke down and Tony got out to fix it. According to Mabel, Frieda screamed at Lawrence, "You're not doing a thing! Why don't you get out and help him?" Lawrence's reply: "I'm a failure as a man in the world of men."

Because the road up the canyon to Taos was a difficult one, they elected to spend the night in Santa Fe, only to find that there were no hotel rooms. Mabel prevailed upon her friend Witter Bynner, the poet, who was living in Santa Fe with the writer and editor Willard "Spud" Johnson, to take them in for the night. At first Lawrence and Bynner were cordial, but they did not like each other. In 1953, Bynner published a somewhat malicious book on Lawrence, entitled *Journey with Genius*, and said of his first meeting with Lawrence that "Lawrence's appearance struck me from the outset as that of a bad baby masquerading as a good Mephistopheles." In a letter to Mabel in 1926, Lawrence described Bynner as "a sort of belated mosquito." Witter Bynner's negative view of Lawrence prompted some Lawrence scholars to call him "Bitter Whiner."

Bynner was, however, immediately drawn to Frieda, with whom he spent much of the night talking, characterizing her as a "household Brunhilde." Meanwhile Mabel took an instant dislike to Frieda, vowing to save Lawrence from her. "Frieda was complete, but limited. Lawrence, tied to her, was incomplete and limited." He was a "lively lamb tied to a solid stake."

When they arrived in Taos the following morning, September 11—Lawrence's thirty-seventh birthday—Frieda and Lawrence were both struck by the beauty of the scene. "In the magnificent fierce morning of New Mexico," Lawrence wrote, "one sprang awake, a new part of the soul woke up suddenly and the old world gave way to the new."[3]

Lawrence wasn't allowed too much time to adjust to living in Taos. After a couple of days, during which the Lawrences stayed in one of Mabel's guest houses, Mabel sent Lawrence off to the Jicarilla Apache reservation with Tony and an old friend from Buffalo, Bessie Wilkinson Freeman. Bessie was a white-haired widow with whom Lawrence immediately established a rapport, maintaining an extensive correspondence with her for many years and visiting her once in Buffalo.

They drove the 120 miles to see the ceremonial dances, an experience Lawrence wrote up in an essay entitled "Indians and an Englishman,"[4] published by *The Dial* in February 1923. In this article, Lawrence described his feelings while watching the Indians perform their ceremony. As in his reaction to the people of Ceylon and the South Sea Islanders, Lawrence noted the immense gulf separating the "civilised" white man from the brown "savage."

When the group returned to Taos after several days, Lawrence found that Mabel and Frieda, despite their initial apathy, had struck up a close relationship, although Mabel had not given up on her plan to "save" Lawrence from Frieda. Lawrence set out immediately on a course to break up this friendly relationship.

THE BURSUM BILL

Although Lawrence could express disdain for the "brown savage," he still had a sense of humanity. He had arrived in Taos at a time when there was great activity surrounding a bill that had been introduced into the U.S. Senate by Senator Holm Olaf Bursum, from New Mexico. The bill, a response to the many battles over land rights among the Anglo settlers, the Hispanics, and the Indians, threatened to grant clear title of Pueblo lands to the Anglos and Hispanics. John Collier, a young poet and educator from New York and California, was a friend of Mabel's and alerted her, and others concerned with Indian rights, to what was happening. He joined Tony Luhan in an active All-Pueblo Council to fight the Bursum Bill. Lawrence could not help but become involved in the cause. As he wrote in an article for the *New York Times* entitled "Certain Americans and an Englishman" (December 24, 1922):

> I arrive in New Mexico at a time of crisis . . .
> The Crisis is a thing called the Bursum Bill, and
> it affects The Pueblo Indians. I wouldn't know
> a thing about it if I needn't, but it's Bursum,
> Bursum, Bursum! The Bill! The Bill, The Bill![5]

His sentence "I wouldn't know a thing about it if I needn't" reflected Lawrence's reluctance to get involved, but he was persuaded by Mabel and Collier to join the cause. Mabel wrote a letter to Lawrence. This letter, dated December 9, 1922, was written on her stationery with the "Las Cruzes, Taos, New Mexico" letterhead crossed out because her mail at times had been wrongly delivered to Las Cruces, New Mexico. "Las Cruzes," meaning "the crosses," was taken from the crosses atop the main building. She wrote that she and Tony had come back to Taos from a trip to Zuni to watch the "Shalico [*sic*] dance" and found a "fearful mail to answer" from all over the country with "questions—demands—resolutions—statements" regarding the Bursum Bill. She added, "This is the first time the country has been appealed to on a question of Indian justice."

A direct appeal is contained in her letter: "Won't you use your great genius at this time to help get something out to the world that will help to make people more conscious of the Indian genius?" Mabel had enlisted the aid of sixty-one prominent artists and writers in her attack on the Bursum Bill, including Carl Sandburg, Zane Grey, Witter Bynner, and Maxfield Parrish. Lawrence, "lamb-like and bewildered," as he described himself, nevertheless wrote the article, which proved to be a very effective statement in opposition. The Bursum Bill was defeated, and in 1924 a more balanced statute, the Pueblo Land Act, was enacted to settle problems of land grants. John Collier continued his work for Indian rights, and in March 1933, President Franklin D. Roosevelt appointed him commissioner of Indian affairs. Albert Fall, the secretary of the interior

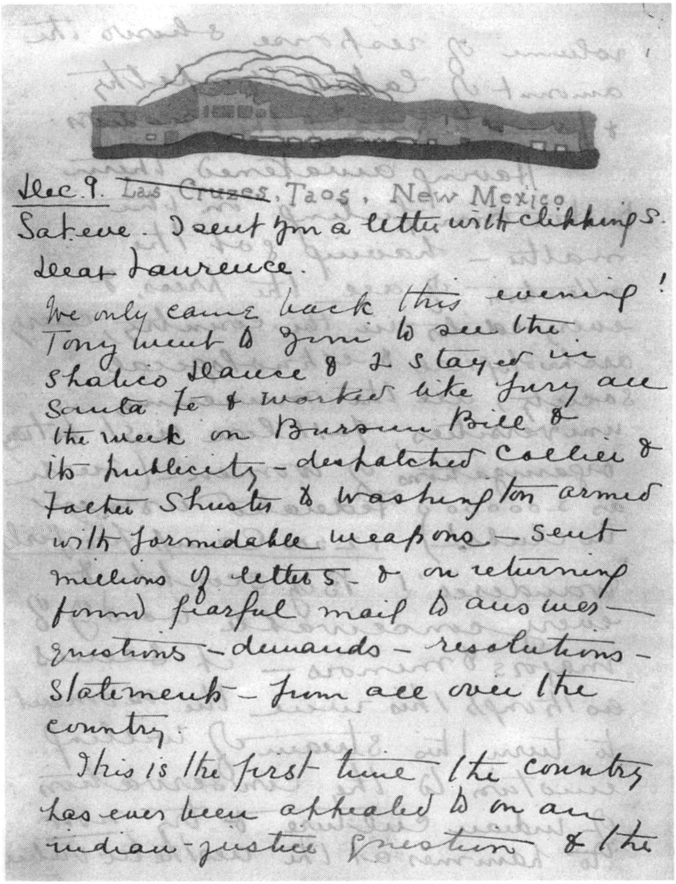

Dec. 9. ~~Las Cruzes~~, Taos, New Mexico
Sat. eve. I sent you a letter with clippings.
Dear Lawrence.
We only came back this evening!
Tony went to Zuni to see the Shalico dance & I stayed in Santa Fe & worked like fury all the week on Bursum Bill & its publicity – despatched Collier & Father Shuster to Washington armed with formidable weapons – sent millions of letters – & on returning found fearful mail to answer – questions – demands – resolutions – statements – from all over the country.
This is the first time the country has ever been appealed to on an indian-justice question & the

Fig. 1. December 9, 1922, letter from Mabel Dodge Luhan to D. H. Lawrence asking for support in attacking the Bursum Bill. Courtesy Richard W. Godin.

who asked Bursum to introduce the bill, was fired by President Garfield.

AN ATTEMPT AT COLLABORATION

About the time the party had come back from the trip to the Jicarilla Apache Reservation, Lawrence suggested to Mabel that they collaborate on a book based on her life, coming from the East as a wealthy patroness and living in the wilds of the West. Lawrence had strong feelings about writing well, but was not averse to collaborating if that was the best way to produce a good work—witness the collaboration in Australia with Mollie Skinner on *The Boy in the Bush*. Lawrence and Mabel began to work on their collaborative effort, choosing the flat roof of Mabel's house as their workplace. At times, Mabel had used this roof, with its view of the mountains and its privacy, to sunbathe in the nude. One can still see the windows Lawrence and Brett colorfully painted, at a later time, screening the roof from Mabel's bedroom.

Frieda did not take kindly to the collaboration and confronted Lawrence with "arms akimbo," saying that if any work were to be done, it would be done in their

Fig. 2. Mabel Dodge Luhan House. Roof shown outside bath area.
All photographs are by Charlotte Page unless otherwise noted.

house. Trying this, Lawrence and Mabel found themselves constantly disrupted by Frieda crashing around the house, sweeping and loudly moving things. Eventually they gave up on the idea. Mabel went on to write a number of books, including the four volumes of her autobiography, *Intimate Memories*, written with the strong encouragement of Lawrence. *Lorenzo in Taos*, while it received mixed reviews (one reviewer said that Mabel had dragged Lawrence's work "through mud, adobe mud"), was a fascinating recollection of the time Lawrence and Frieda spent in Taos. The book, interestingly enough, was written loosely in the form of a letter to the poet Robinson Jeffers, wishing he had met Lawrence and telling him of the experiences she had with Lawrence and Frieda.

Lawrence wrote about the guesthouse in which they were quartered:

> The big house is about 200 yards away—an adobe pile. I don't like very much being on the grounds of a *padrona* but Mabel Sterne is quite generous. . . . Whether I *really* like it is another matter. It is all an experience. But one's heart is never

Fig. 3. Mabel Dodge Luhan guesthouse on ranch: Tony's house, used by Lawrences. Courtesy Suazo Family, Taos Pueblo.

touched at all—neither by landscape, Indians, or Americans.[6]

During his stay at the guest house, Lawrence was characteristically contradictory, expressing disdain for the "arty" community of Taos (Taos, he once said, is "so much artistic small beer") but then complaining that Mabel didn't invite people for him to meet. When there were social gatherings, Lawrence and Frieda were often unruly in their behavior, carrying their frequent domestic battles into a public arena. One evening Lawrence reportedly screamed at Frieda, "Take that dirty cigarette out of your mouth! And stop sticking out that fat belly of yours!" Frieda replied, "You'd better stop that talk or I'll tell about *your* things!"[7] A few minutes later, the guests were astonished to see Frieda and Lawrence strolling arm in arm in the moonlight.

This complex love/hate relationship seemed characteristic of the Lawrences' interaction. Frieda herself commented, during a conference panel about Lawrence held at UCLA in 1972:

> When I wanted to be disagreeable and say something nasty, it didn't work, and when I said something quite innocent he got mad.[8]

After Lawrence's death, Frieda was involved in legal actions with Lawrence's family. According to Robert Lucas, Witter Bynner reported an incident in the courtroom in which Frieda's attorney tried to portray a blissful marital relationship, whereupon Frieda stood up and exclaimed, "Oh, but no! That's not true! We fought like hell!"—much to the amusement of the court.[9]

Unfortunately, the story may not be true. T. H. Huxley once wrote that many a beautiful theory is ruined by an ugly fact. Lucas writes that what really happened is that Frieda explained that she and Lawrence had a deep understanding, but they "did, of course, quarrel now and then."[10]

Brett told of times when Lawrence lost his temper. On one occasion, Bill and Rachel Hawk, from the neighboring Del Monte Ranch, came over to the Lawrences' cabin for dinner, which was not going well owing to a recalcitrant chicken. Enraged, Lawrence stormed around the kitchen and tried to restore order, then calmed down. Brett also recounts a time in London when an angry Lawrence took a poker and, with a sweep of his arm, destroyed a tea set resting on a tabletop. Longtime Taos resident and writer/photographer Mildred Tolbert recalls Brett retelling the story in her later years in Taos, complete with poker and sweeping gestures, but lacking the doomed tea set.

The incident of the poker and the tea set is also recounted by Joseph Foster, who tells of the time in Lawrence's flat in London when a number of his friends, including J. Middleton Murry, S. S. Koteliansky, and Brett, were there. As Foster says, "Lawrence talked constantly," until "Suddenly Frieda began attacking him, then denouncing him, finally accusing him of wanting to make a God of himself." Lawrence grew angrier, and "Suddenly he seized the poker and started breaking the cups and saucers. 'Beware, Frieda. If ever you talk to me like that again it will not be tea things smashed, but your head. Oh, yes. I will kill you. So beware.'" And he smashed the teapot with the poker.[11]

That the Lawrences "did quarrel now and then" is not in dispute. That they also had a loving dependency upon one another is also true.

THE HAWKS' RANCH

Frieda and Lawrence began to chafe at their proximity to Mabel, and in a letter to Bessie Freeman, dated October 31, 1922, six weeks after they had arrived in Taos, Lawrence wrote that they were interested in moving to the ranch owned by John Evans (Mabel's son), about twenty miles up in the mountains. But in a letter dated November 14, also to Freeman, he wrote that the cabin they wanted to rent had been broken into, and the repairs needed precluded any chance of their spending the winter there.

Fig. 4. Del Monte cabin, Lawrences sitting on front porch. Courtesy
Keith Sagar.

They did have another opportunity when Alfred Decker
Hawk, whose ranch, the Del Monte, adjoined that of
Evans, offered them a cabin to rent, which they took.

They left the guesthouse, which Mabel had provided
for Tony, and on November 30, 1922, Lawrence wrote
letters to Mabel and Tony and left them on the table in
the big house while Mabel and Tony were off in Santa
Fe. To Mabel, he wrote that he had left everything in the
guesthouse except for a few items such as some blankets
he wanted to borrow. To Tony, he wrote:

Dear Tony:

Thank you so much for letting us live in your house. I hope you won't find it much the worse for wear. Let me give you a few for its christening. Come over soon to see us at Lobo.

Yrs,

D. H. Lawrence[12]

On December 9, Tony dictated a letter to Mabel for her to write to Lawrence in which he returned the check for the rent money. The letter is on the same stationery Mabel used to write Lorenzo about the Bursum Bill (page 17) with the "Las Cruzes, Taos, New Mexico" letterhead, but this time the "Las Cruzes" is not crossed out—which, as noted earlier, Mabel did because her mail was sometimes delivered to Las Cruces, New Mexico. The letter begins:

Dear Lorenzo:

I am very glad you gave me that money. I didn't mean to ask you anything for staying in my house but I didn't mean to ask anything because I been very glad to see using my house. Mabel—I

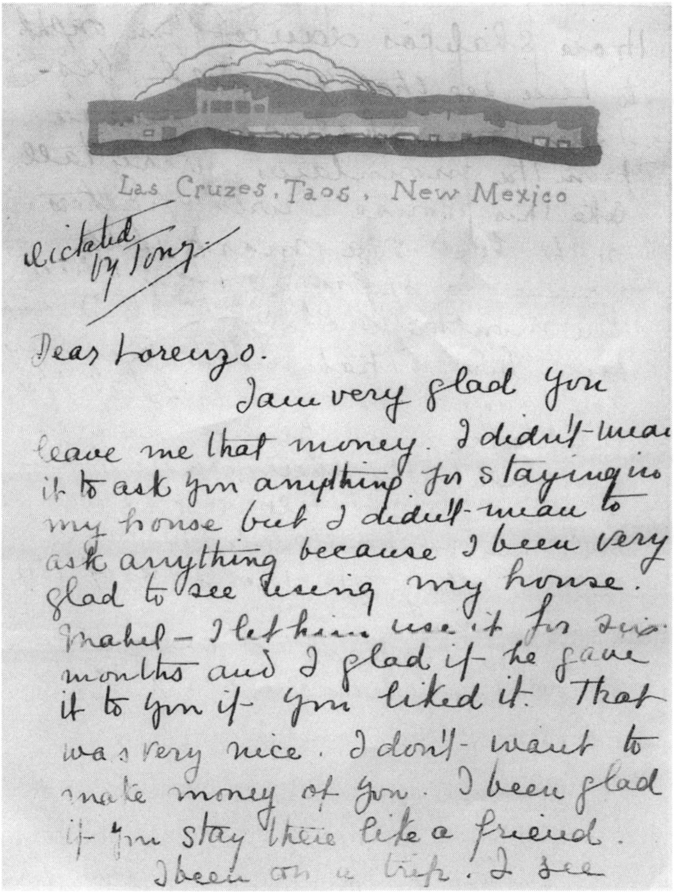

Las Cruzes, Taos, New Mexico

dictated
by Tony

Dear Lorenzo.

I am very glad you leave me that money. I didn't mean it to ask you anything for staying in my house but I didn't mean to ask anything because I been very glad to see using my house. Mabel — I let him use it for two months and I glad if he gave it to you if you liked it. That was very nice. I don't want to make money of you. I been glad if you stay there like a friend. I been on a trip. I see

Fig. 5. February 9, 1922, letter to Lawrence, dictated by Tony to Mabel Dodge Luhan. Courtesy Richard W. Godin.

let him use it for six months and if he gave it to you if he liked it. That was very nice. I don't want to make money of you. I been glad if you stay there like a friend.[13]

After telling Lorenzo of their trip to see the Shalicos [*sic*] at Zuni, Tony returns to the question of the rent money, dictating to Mabel:

I guess you going to say I don't take the check because I don't like the money ways & I don't need it but that's not true. It's because I want it to be friends & not money ways.[14]

The letter was signed, also in Mabel's hand, "Su Amigo, Antonio Lujan" (the Spanish spelling of "Luhan").

So the Lawrences vacated Tony's house and moved up to the Del Monte Ranch, where they rented the cabin. Figure 4 shows the Lawrences on the cabin porch. Lawrence described it as "an old log-house with five rooms, very primitive."[15]

Some confusion about the ranch appears on occasion.

Fig. 6. Del Monte cabin, present day.

Eliot Fay, in his book on Lawrence, says that Mabel owned the Del Monte Ranch and that it was managed for her by the Hawks.[16] Alfred Decker Hawk and his wife, Lucy, owned the ranch. Their son Bill and his wife, Rachel, lived on it with their son, Walton, who still lives in this cabin (see fig. 6). Brett took a photo of Lawrence on Frieda's horse, Azul, with two-year-old Walton Hawk astride in front of him (fig. 7). Brett later wrote:

Suddenly you take Walton by the shoulders and draw him toward you. You hold him between your knees and look at him intently. Your eyes are a deep blue. . . . The child stares back at you solemnly and puts up a hand to stroke your beard. You release him at last with a sigh.[17]

Brett was an accomplished artist and did a woodblock depicting Lawrence on horseback in a position similar to the photograph she took of Lawrence and the young Walton Hawk. The woodblock (fig. 8) appeared in the September 1930 (no. 18) issue of Spud Johnson's magazine, *Laughing Horse*. Figure 9 is a recent photograph of Walton Hawk. The Lawrences became friends with the younger Hawks, Bill and Rachel, although Walton has said that his mother did not entirely like Lawrence because she was a fine horsewoman and he was hard on horses, riding them roughly.[18] Lawrence had been taught to ride by Tony and Mabel and enjoyed it, but he could be overly taxing on his mounts.

The Lawrences rode frequently and were often joined by friends on their rides. Dorothy Brandenburg, daughter of the Taos artist Oscar Berninghaus and a longtime

Fig. 7. D. H. Lawrence on Frieda's horse, "Azul," with
two-year-old Walton Hawk. Photograph by Dorothy Brett.
Courtesy Walton Hawk.

resident of Taos, was born in 1902, and was in her twenties when she rode up to the Kiowa Ranch to ride with the Lawrences. She may have been the only remaining person in Taos, and perhaps the world, who actually knew Lawrence. She recalled one ride when Frieda was overlong in preparing for the ride, leaving the others outside growing impatient. She finally appeared, wearing a bright green dress with a wide collar. Dorothy recalled the image: "She came out wearing this lettuce-green dress, her cheeks rosy-red, her hair the bright color of Mayonnaise." Dorothy remembered everyone looking at Frieda, and Lawrence exclaiming, "My God, Woman! You look like a salad!"[19]

THE DANISH ARTISTS

Walter Ufer, a prominent member of the Taos Society of Artists, had introduced the Lawrences to two Danish artists, Knud Merrild and Kai Götzsche, both of whom the Lawrences liked. Lawrence had gone camping with the Danes. They all agreed that the Danes should rent a cabin on the Hawks's ranch near the one the Lawrences had rented. Cushman writes of the strong interest Lawrence took in helping the Danes.[20] He wrote to his publisher,

Salute, Lorenzo!   *Dorothy Brett*

Fig. 8. Woodblock by Dorothy
Brett, *Salute Lorenzo!*

Fig. 9. Walton Hawk,
recent photograph.

Thomas Seltzer, that he would like Merrild to do dust-jacket illustrations. He is, Lawrence wrote, "a clever decorator." Seltzer did use one illustration for the jacket of Lawrence's novella *The Captain's Doll*.

Merrild later wrote about their experiences in a book entitled *A Poet and Two Painters*, a later version (1974) published under the title *With D. H. Lawrence in New Mexico*. They spent a harsh winter, frozen in and suffering from severe temperatures—such as 25 degrees below zero on February 10, 1923—but the Danes and the Lawrences managed well, doing their own carpentry, splitting logs, and melting snow for drinking water. All this was a far cry from the life Lawrence and Frieda had known. The Danes painted while Lawrence composed a series of poems to complete the collection to be published as *Birds, Beasts and Flowers*, as well as finishing his *Studies in Classic American Literature*.

LAKE CHAPALA, MEXICO

On March 18, 1923, the Lawrences left the Danes in their cabin, hoping that they would follow them to old Mexico. The Lawrences arrived in Mexico City in March, traveled around Mexico, and by April had settled on Lake Chapala. They were joined by Witter Bynner and Willard "Spud" Johnson.

While in Mexico, Lawrence finished a draft of *The Plumed Serpent*, which he had begun at the ranch. The title of the novel at that time was *Quetzalcoatl*, named after the legendary ruler of the Toltec in Mexico. The publisher changed the name, leading Lawrence to observe that it sounded like millinery.

In July 1923, Lawrence and Frieda traveled to New York, via New Orleans, to stay with Lawrence's American publishers, Thomas and Adele Seltzer. The Seltzers rented a cottage in New Jersey where Lawrence could work in quiet. By August, Frieda was ready to go to Europe. Frieda had long wanted to return to Europe, and to visit her children in England and her mother in Germany, but Lawrence was reluctant to go back. His refusal to return to Europe with her hurt and infuriated Frieda. Lawrence wrote to Amy Lowell on August 18, the day Frieda sailed, that he needed "to get away from people altogether. That is why I can't go to Europe." He felt the demands upon him would have been enormous.

Lawrence left New York to visit Bessie Freeman in Buffalo—Mabel's friend with whom he had visited the Jicarilla Apache when he first arrived in Taos in 1922, and with whom he had kept up a correspondence. He also went to see Mabel's mother and had lunch with her at Niagara Falls.

Then Lawrence took the train to Los Angeles to join up with the two Danes, Merrild and Götzsche, who had been living and working there. Lawrence arrived on August 30. He enjoyed his stay, but was distressed by his separation from Frieda. He and Götzsche went to Mexico, wandered along the western coast, and eventually went to Guadalajara. Lawrence found Mexico a disappointment, seeing unwelcome changes in his charming Chapala, which may have been partly due to his sadness at being separated from Frieda. Frieda had written and cabled him to come and join her, and on November 22, Lawrence and Götzsche set sail on the SS *Toledo* from Vera Cruz— Lawrence to England, Götzsche to Denmark. Lawrence soon regretted it:

[I] hate England—feel like an animal in a trap.

It all seems so dead and dark and buried. . . . I want to get back west.—Taos is heaven in comparison.[21]

LONDON AND "THE LAST SUPPER"

While in London, Lawrence organized a dinner party at the Café Royal, which was called "The Last Supper." He invited seven of his friends, including John Middleton Murry, the Carswells, and Dorothy Brett. Lawrence proposed that they all return with him to the ranch in Taos and start a utopian colony, "Rananim." By the end of the dinner party, virtually every guest, save Mary Cannan, agreed to follow Lawrence to New Mexico and start the ideal colony, but when it came to the actual packing for the departure, there was only one recruit—the Honorable Dorothy Brett.

The three—Lawrence, Frieda, and Brett—arrived in Taos the third week of March 1924. Brett, a trained artist, was young and very deaf, using an ear trumpet she named "Toby," an instrument that irritated Mabel but fascinated the Pueblo Indians. Lawrence used Brett and her hearing device in a short story, "The Last Laugh," in which young, deaf Miss James uses a "Marconi listening machine."

Fig. 10. Young Dorothy Brett. Photograph by Witter Bynner.
Courtesy Richard W. Godin.

As the daughter of a viscount, Dorothy had the courtesy title of "Honorable." Her sister, the Honorable Sylvia Brooke, married an Englishman appointed to be the last white rajah of Borneo, making Sylvia the Ranee of Sarawak. She wrote a delightful autobiography, *Queen of the Headhunters*, telling the story and also providing an interesting account of her growing up, with Dorothy Brett, in the rather dysfunctional family of Viscount Esher.

Rananim, a name apparently derived from a Hebrew song that Lawrence's friend S. S. Koteliansky had sung to him, was used to describe his concept of an ideal community, first used in a letter dated January 3, 1915, to Koteliansky. In his letter, he also discussed using the image of a phoenix rising as an emblem: "an eagle . . . or a phoenix, argent, rising from a flaming nest of scarlet, on a black background." He called the society "The Order of The Knights of Rananim," and even designed a flag like that on a pirate vessel, "a blazing, ten-pointed star, scarlet on a black background." These designs appear to derive from a phoenix rising from flames in a thirteenth-century illustration from "The Ashmolean Bestiary," at the Bodleian Library, Oxford University.

Lawrence often revived this utopian idea, including in an invitation to Merrild and Götzsche to follow him and Frieda to Mexico, where they would start their own community. ⌐

CHAPTER THREE

Taos II

March to October 1924

The Lawrences returned to Taos, this time with Dorothy Brett. This, his second stay in Taos, was the most productive writing period of all Lawrence's visits.

They were once again guests of Mabel. Across from the big house, in the alfalfa field, was the adobe structure "Pink House," one of the buildings Mabel had constructed. A minor bit of confusion exists with regard to the decorating of the house. Fay writes, "Mabel was preparing her small 'Pink House' . . . for the arrival of a friend named Alice Sprague. Lawrence suggested that all of them set to work to decorate it."[1] But Brett writes, "Today we are busy painting the little pink house that Mrs. Sprague had."[2] Before or after, one thing is certain: the three—Lawrence, Frieda, and Brett—set to an exuberant job of decorating. Frieda painted a walnut chest of drawers pale pink, with handles that had carved grapes painted purple and green. Brett did an apple tree, serpent, and Adam and Eve on the lower half of the front door. Her figures had movable stick arms. Lawrence placed his phoenix rising from the flames on the door's upper half, and on the outside bathroom door he painted a huge sunflower, a green snake wrapped around its base, surrounded by a plate-sized black butterfly, a white dove, a brown bullfrog, and a rooster.

For a while, the Lawrences, Brett, and Mabel got along well, but tensions gradually built. One evening Mabel had invited Brett to dinner, which she declined; later, Mabel found them all seated at dinner in the guest house. Brett, in her book *Lawrence and Brett: A Friendship*, describes the incident, using her characteristic historical-present style:

> In she walks, without speaking or looking at us, and sits down on the day-bed. Not a word is spoken by any of us. She leans back, silent, like a stone monument. We look at each other. . . . Frieda's eyes are blazing, and you look down at your plate, entirely withdrawn. . . . At last, as suddenly as she came, she gets up and goes. Frieda gives a nervous

Fig. 11. "Pink House." Courtesy Kevin Cannon.

giggle, but you are cold with anger. . . . I feel an undercurrent of emotional strain.[3]

THE KIOWA RANCH

Mabel, in a burst of generosity (and probably to keep Lawrence in Taos), offered Lawrence a tract of 160 acres on her ranch, which adjoined the Del Monte Ranch. Lawrence refused, so Mabel tendered the offer to Frieda, who accepted. The deed was in Frieda's name. The ranch was the only home the Lawrences ever owned. Years later, Frieda purchased a home in Texas as a retreat from the winter, as well as a home on Taos Mesa to be nearer the town.

There is some question as to whether Lawrence or Frieda actually made the deal with Mabel to give her the manuscript of *Sons and Lovers* in return for the gift of the ranch, but it was done. Mabel, it has been reported, later gave the manuscript to her psychoanalyst, A. A. Brill, as payment on a bill incurred by a friend.

THE HISTORY OF THE RANCH

In October 1883, John and Louise Craig acquired the land on which the ranch stands under the Homestead Act of 1862. It is believed that John built the cabin in which the Lawrences lived during their stays, and it was always referred to as "The Homesteader's Cabin." The ranch is located near Lobo Mountain in San Cristobal, some twenty miles north of Taos, at an elevation of 8,500 feet (1,500 feet higher than Taos).

In 1893 the Craigs sold the property to William and Mary McClure. The McClures established the alfalfa field in front, which was still thriving when the Lawrences lived there. Lawrence used the alfalfa field as a setting in his novella *St. Mawr*:

> The alfalfa field was one raging, seething conflict of plants. . . . the rush of red sparks and michael-mas daisies, and the tough wild sunflowers, stran-gling and choking the dark tender green of the clover-like alfalfa! A battle, a battle with banners of bright scarlet and yellow.[4]

At the time, the ranch was called "The Flying Heart." The McClures also raised a herd of some five hundred white Angora goats, a fact that apparently remained with Lawrence, who named the New Mexico mountain ranch Lou Witt bought in *St. Mawr* "Las Chivas," Spanish for "female goats." Mabel Dodge Luhan bought the ranch in May 1920 for $1,500 and gave it to her only child, John Evans, who used it primarily for hunting. In 1922, Mabel bought the ranch back from Evans for a buffalo-hide coat and a small amount of cash. The Lawrences first named the ranch the "Lobo Ranch," from the nearby mountain (*lobo* being Spanish for "wolf"), but later changed it to the "Kiowa Ranch," presumably because the Kiowa Indians were known to have used a trail to the mountains that went through the ranch property. The ranch remained the "Kiowa" until the 1950s, when the University of New Mexico accepted it as a gift from Frieda and renamed it "The D. H. Lawrence Ranch," as it is still called.

THE LAWRENCES TAKE OVER THE RANCH

When the Lawrences took over the ranch property, the cabins on the ranch were in a dilapidated, unlivable state, so Lawrence, with the help of Taos Pueblo Indians Candido, Geronimo, and Trinidad, and Brett, worked diligently to repair the homes, dig an irrigation ditch, and clean out the well. Frieda cooked for the crews. Lawrence worked hard, as hard as any of the workers. In a bucolic mood, he bought a cow he named "Black-Eyed Susan," a cock named "Moses," and a flock of hens.

THE D. H. LAWRENCE RANCH TODAY

In 2003, the D. H. Lawrence Society of North America submitted a proposal to the Cultural Properties Review

Committee of New Mexico for historic registry of the ranch, a proposal that was unanimously approved and forwarded with recommendation for National Historic Register and National Historic Landmark status. The National Register of Historic Places entered the ranch into the registry in January 2004. The comprehensive proposal was supported by many members of the society and was prepared by Tina Ferris and Virginia Hyde. New assessments, measurements, and other records were necessary for this proposal, and many details in the following descriptions of the ranch come from this extensive document.[5]

The Caretaker's Cabin

As a visitor enters the ranch, the first building to be seen by the parking lot is the caretaker's cabin. It is used as a ranch office and home for the caretaker, Al Bearce, who has been managing the ranch for the University of New Mexico since the 1950s. The welcoming dogs are his. This is a two-story building of log construction. It was built after the original two-room guest cabin was torn down in 1933, and was used by Frieda Lawrence and Angelo Ravagli as a residence. It is L-shaped, with a single-story extension.

The "Homesteader's Cabin," in which the Lawrences lived, is a three-room dwelling, built by Craig around 1891. It is uphill and approximately forty feet east of the caretaker's cabin, and measures 42 x 14 feet. An adobe-brick fireplace was added later on. There are two entrances in the front of the cabin, one leading to the west room, which Lawrence used as a bedroom, and the other opening into the east room, used as a kitchen and dining room.

On the porch, Lawrence's wooden armchair still sits. In the middle is a sitting room, with a 6 1/2 x 4-foot, twenty-four-paned window that provided the Lawrences with a view of the alfalfa field as well as a magnificent view of the mountains to the west. It was also used as Frieda's bedroom.

Additional improvements and restoration were done by the Lawrences, by Frieda during the 1930s (such as the addition of a modern kitchen), and, over the years, by the University of New Mexico.

Prominent on the outside west wall of the cabin is a painting of a buffalo done by Lawrence's Taos Indian helper and friend Trinidad Archuleta, four years after Lawrence's death. For the Taos Indians, the buffalo

Fig. 12. D. H. Lawrence Ranch office, present day.

Fig. 13. D. H. Lawrence Ranch, Homesteader's Cabin, present day.

was—as Collier noted—"a tranquil giant, loved and not feared."[6] Trinidad painted the buffalo and signed it, in bold, charming phonetics, "TRNDOD ARCHULETA 1934." In the 1950s, Trinidad returned to the ranch and restored the painting, which unfortunately stands in need of further work at present.

Figure 14 shows the side of the Homesteader's Cabin, where Trinidad's painting may barely be seen, with a view of Brett's cabin, showing the proximity to the Homesteader's Cabin.

Brett's Cabin

Dorothy Brett's cabin is a closed-in, 9 x 11-foot structure, similar in construction to the Homesteader's Cabin, made of log and adobe plaster. It stands about forty-five feet northwest of the main cabin, and as the other cabin does, it faces south. It is built on a slope, and the east window sits a mere eight inches from the ground. When the Lawrences were away, or in the winter, Brett often lived in a more commodious cabin offered her by the Hawk family on their neighboring Del Monte Ranch. Brett seemed not to mind the close quarters. She could have chosen to live in

Fig. 14. Side view of Homesteader's Cabin. Brett's cabin at left rear.

the larger, two-room guest cabin—which at the time was where the caretaker's cabin now stands—but the guest cabin stood in a grove of trees and was too gloomy. She explained to Lawrence that she preferred the smaller cabin: "It's quite big enough, really, and I like the sunlight."[7] In it she typed many of Lawrence's manuscripts, and the little round table and typewriter she is believed to have used are still in place. On this typewriter Brett typed, among other manuscripts, the texts of *St. Mawr* and *The Woman Who Rode Away*. It is also likely to be the typewriter Aldous

Fig. 15. Typewriter in Brett's cabin today, possibly used by Brett to type Lawrence's manuscripts.

Huxley used in an account related by Paul Horgan, who tells of a visit to the ranch in 1937. He was invited by Frieda to join a party for lunch. As he and Frieda were walking past the cabin in which Aldous and Maria Huxley were staying, he heard the sounds of a typewriter. The sound caused Frieda a moment of sadness, which she explained by telling Horgan that Huxley was going blind and practiced typing in the dark so he could continue writing after he was unable to see.[8]

[Facing page] Fig. 16. "The Lawrence Tree."

The "Lawrence Tree"

Directly in front of the Homesteader's Cabin, around twenty-five feet to the east, stands a large ponderosa pine. Under this tree rested a simple bench on which Lawrence would sit and write. The bench was used by Georgia O'Keeffe to create her oil painting of the tree in 1929. Lying on her back, she painted the tree at a soaring angle, a nighttime view with a starry sky. The painting now resides in the Wadsworth Athenaeum in Hartford, Connecticut.

The tree was a most significant part of Lawrence's life on the ranch. In his essay "A Little Moonshine with Lemon," Lawrence writes, "Perhaps when I have any *Weh* [sadness] at all, my *heimweh* [homesickness] is for the tree in front of the house."[9] Pines figured prominently in his stories written in New Mexico, *St. Mawr* and *The Woman Who Rode Away*. In his essay "Pan in America," he writes, "Here, on this little ranch under the Rocky Mountains, a big pine tree rises like a guardian spirit in front of the cabin where we live," and endows the tree, which "long, long ago the Indians blazed," with the wild spirit of Pan.[10]

The Memorial

The Lawrence Memorial is sometimes grandiloquently called "The Shrine," which Frieda had not intended when she had Angelo Ravagli build it. They usually referred to it as "The Chapel." It lies to the northeast of the main buildings, up a steep, winding path. Built in 1934 by Angelo, it is a small building measuring 12 x 15 feet. White-plastered, the building is made of adobe bricks, cement, and wood, with a gabled roof made of cedar-shake shingles. In front of the memorial, on the peak of the roof, sits a carving of a phoenix, Lawrence's symbol of death and rebirth. The phoenix measures two feet. Beneath it is a rosette window constructed from a farmer's wheel. Two *bancos*, shallow walls, extend out from the building.

The interior of the memorial is very much a chapel; centered in the back of the memorial is the altar, upon which visitors from all over the world leave tokens of esteem and respect, such as flowers. The altar measures 43 x 20 x 22 inches high, has "DHL" carved on the front, and is decorated with leaves and sunflowers.

The guest book, which stands at the north wall, has signatures and comments from these visitors, usually

Fig. 17. D. H. Lawrence Memorial.

laudatory of the writer whose memorial they have come to visit. Above the guest book is a certificate of Lawrence's cremation, and permission to transport the ashes issued by the French government and signed in grand style by the "Directeur des Pompes Funèbres [Director of Morticians], la Port de Marseilles."

Lawrence's ashes were brought to Taos by Ravagli in 1935, and he had some difficulty with U.S. Customs in New York, which was soon resolved. Frieda claimed to

Fig. 18. Interior of D. H. Lawrence Memorial.

have mixed Lawrence's ashes in the cement of the altar, to protect them. More on the interment of the ashes and the dedication of the memorial will be found on page 99–104.

The wall of the plastered memorial interior, measuring nine-and-a-half feet in height, is painted yellow. Exposed joists are painted blue and silver. An iron chandelier, Spanish in style, hangs from the ceiling. From above, a rosette window, painted with a sunflower and measuring thirty inches across, lights the altar.

Other Structures

Other buildings on the ranch are the horse corral (originally used by the McClures for keeping their goats), two log barns, and a covered cow shed. The larger barn is situated about ten feet southwest of Brett's cabin and measures 32 x 18 feet. It has an entrance on the east side, but no windows. To the northwest of Brett's cabin sits a smaller barn, used by the Lawrences as a chicken coop. This barn faces south and measures approximately 11 x 13 feet. It has six paned windows over the entryway. Angelo added onto the smaller barn in the 1930s, an addition to the west measuring 24 x 25 feet.

The corral, used by the McClures to keep goats, lies in a clearing around one hundred feet to the northwest of the chicken coop. It measures 42 x 56 feet with its covered stable. The stable has four stalls, each one fourteen feet deep, with three of them open to the west and one enclosed as a tack area. This is where the Lawrences kept their horses.

While the crew was working on the ranch, the Pueblo Indians camped above the cabins. Mabel and Tony also set up a tepee, and Mabel pitched in by running into Taos for needed supplies. It was in general a happy time, although strenuous both in hard labor and in interpersonal relationships. Frieda and Lawrence had some tension between them, and the triangle of Frieda, Brett, and Lawrence wore on Frieda at times. Brett reports that the Pueblo Indians got along very well with Lawrence and called him "Red Fox," presumably because of his flaming beard.[11] Bynner thought the nickname was "Red Wolf," and it is probable that both might have been used. Brett also notes that the nickname they had for Frieda was "Angry Winter."

Brett commented on the discussions they had in the evenings in the cabin, noting that Lawrence seemed to be in one of his moods of condemnation.[12] Lawrence, the author who championed freedom to write in his essay "Pornography and Obscenity," and who had himself been attacked and had his works suppressed as obscene, declaimed that the last part of James Joyce's *Ulysses* "is the dirtiest, most indecent, obscene thing ever written. . . . It is filthy."

Lawrence was often up at five, chasing Susan, the cow. Working on cupboards and baking bread in the *horno* built by one of his Taos Indian helpers, Lawrence did the housework and taught Frieda, of a more aristocratic background, many household tasks. Trinidad's wife, Rufina, worked as an aide to Frieda, until they had a row and Rufina departed.

Frieda churned butter, and all in all, it seemed a healthy existence. Lawrence began to write once more, slipping off into the woods to work on his novella *St. Mawr.* ⌒

CHAPTER FOUR

Lawrence's Writings in Taos

March to October 1924

During the period from March to October 1924, Lawrence was active in his writing. Among the major works he produced during this period were the essays "Pan in America" and "The Hopi Snake Dance," and the short fiction pieces *St. Mawr*, "The Princess," and "The Woman Who Rode Away." He also began writing *The Plumed Serpent*.

The three works of fiction—"The Princess," "The Woman Who Rode Away," and *St. Mawr*—all have an element in common: the stark mountains of New Mexico, which provide a critical backdrop (although in "The Woman Who Rode Away," the stark mountain backdrop is transferred to Old Mexico). There is also the theme of rich white women—two American, one British—who end up degraded, alienated, or (literally) sacrificed.

Lawrence himself, in a letter to Catherine Carswell (October 8, 1924) wrote:

It is also very hard living against these savage Rockies. The savage things are a bit gruesome, and they try to down one.—But far better they than the white disintegration—I did a long novelette . . . about 2 women and a horse—'St. Mawr.' . . . And two shorter novelettes . . . 'The Woman Who Rode Away' and 'The Princess.' 'St. Mawr' ends here. They are all about this country more or less. . . . They are all sad. After all, they're true to what is.[1]

"THE PRINCESS"

The protagonist in "The Princess" is an Englishwoman, Mary Henrietta Urquhart, generally considered an imaginative portrait of Brett. Her father calls her "My Princess," while her mother calls her "My Dollie." Her relatives in Boston refer to her as "Dollie Urqhuart, poor little thing." "She was always grown up, she never really grew up. Always strangely wise and always childish." Dollie's father, the "old Celtic hero" Colin, dies, and she moves to America with her father's nurse, Charlotte Cummins. They move to a dude ranch in New Mexico,

"El Rancho del Cerro Gordo" (Fat Hill), where they meet Domingo Romero, the scion of an old San Cristobal family whose wealth has gone, reducing him to the status of a peasant. Dollie, Charlotte, and Domingo ride on horseback up into the deep, stark mountains. Charlotte turns back, leaving Dollie and Domingo by themselves to ride up to the distant cabin. Once there, Dollie and Domingo find the cabin in bad condition, offering poor protection. That night, Dollie complains of being cold and Domingo comes into her bed to warm her, "with a terrible animal warmth that seemed to annihilate her." Dollie, portrayed as a frigid woman bound by snobbish principles of aristocracy, is reduced to hysterics, feeling trapped and degraded. A team of forest rangers appear to "free" her, and engage in a gunfire battle in which Domingo is killed. Some time later, Dollie marries an older man, with the implication that she has regained her father.

Lawrence continues this theme of degradation in a short piece written after he had returned to Europe in 1925, a story called "None of That." This is the story of a rich American woman who comes to Mexico. Unlike the passive

Dollie, this woman seeks men who have a "dramatic sort of power," her own power over men making them "dance like marionettes in a tragi-comedy." Lawrence makes it clear that her power works on European and American men, but Mexican men avoid her. When men want to possess her, she remarks, "I'm having none of that," whence the title. She is attracted to a Mexican bullfighter who offers an erotic challenge of power. He turns her over to six of his assistants, who rape her, leaving her degraded and in a state of nervous collapse, powerless. Several days later, she dies.

Lawrence used a similar theme in his well-known short-fiction piece "The Woman Who Rode Away," whose protagonist is generally thought to be Mabel Dodge Luhan. It was written between the two halves of *The Plumed Serpent* and reflects similar thematic material, involving ancient Mexican religion.

"THE WOMAN WHO RODE AWAY"

The protagonist in "The Woman Who Rode Away" is an American woman from California, married to a mining engineer who "downed her, kept her in invisible slavery."

His search for silver takes them into the Sierra Madre mountains of Mexico. When the silver doesn't pan out, he tries farming, but the quest for silver is always dominant. A chance conversation with two visiting mining engineers, who tell about a tribe of Indians ("descendants of Montezuma and the old Aztec or Totonac kings") living deep in the mountains and practicing ancient religion, stirs a desire in her to ride into the mountains. She rides alone on a grueling journey of three days through difficult terrain and encounters two young Indians who ask her where she is going. "I want to visit the Chilchui Indians . . . to know their Gods." "Chilchui" is apparently Lawrence's alteration of the real Huichol Indians of that area. The Indians take her to their site. Humiliating her along the way by making her horse bolt, jerking her forward, and requiring her to crawl across a narrow ledge while they walk erect, they finally arrive at the Chilchui camp. They appear before the elder, the cacique, whose face "was so old, it was like dark glass." She is taken away and told to take her clothes off, which she refuses to do, whereupon her clothes are slit and removed. She is given new clothes to wear: a white cotton shift and a blue woolen tunic embroidered with scarlet and green flowers—blue, the color of the wind, the color of death.

The woman, who is never named, is given potions of honey and herbs that produce vomiting, but also a languor and a sense of heightened perception—she can feel "the sound of evening flowers unfolding." She is bathed in oil and prepared for a sacrifice, which is part of the regeneration of the world. "When a white woman sacrifices herself to our gods, then our gods will begin to make the world again, and the white men's gods will fall to pieces."

She is taken into a mountain cave, stripped, and placed on a flat stone altar for the ritual. The priest, killing her with his knife, strikes at the very moment the setting sun shines through the shaft of ice at the mouth of the cave.

The cave has an interesting history. One afternoon in May, Mabel and Tony led Lawrence, Frieda, and Brett on horseback to an Indian ceremonial cave in the mountains behind Arroyo Seco. The cave was beautiful, very high, with a waterfall cascading down the entrance. In the final paragraphs of "The Woman Who Rode Away," Lawrence wrote:

Then through the bushes she emerged into a strange amphitheatre. Facing was a great wall of hollow rock, down the front of which hung a great, dripping, fang-like spoke of ice.[2]

The cave is still behind Arroyo Seco, with the fanglike spoke of ice clearly visible in the winter, a gushing waterfall other times of the year. Lawrence's description, as always, is wonderfully accurate. Figure 19 is a photograph of the cave in winter.

St. Mawr

The story of *St. Mawr* is in itself a social commentary, contrasting the "little, old, unreal" Shropshire landscape with the wilderness of America.

St. Mawr's protagonist is Louise (Lou) Witt, an American, married to Sir Henry Carrington, known as "Rico." Rico is an effete dilettante whom Lou sees as "poor old Rico, going on like an amiable machine from day to day." Rico's sexless, powerless nature is brought into sharp focus for Lou when she meets St. Mawr, a powerful stallion, and sees that "the black, fiery flow in

the eyes of the horse was something much more terri-
fing and real, the only thing that was real." Rico is injured
in an accident in which St. Mawr falls on him, owing to
Rico's own fault. Rico wants to have St. Mawr destroyed
or gelded. Lou and her mother, Rachel Witt, defend
St. Mawr—Rachel saying, "I will preserve one last male
thing in the museum of this world, if I can."[3]

Brett, in her book *Lawrence and Brett: A Friendship*,
relates an interesting story about *St. Mawr*. She tells of
a moment when Lawrence was reading aloud to Frieda
and Brett from *St. Mawr*, on which he was then working.
Brett writes about Lawrence's reading of the accident to
Rico, addressing Lawrence: "You read it with such keen joy
and pleasure at the final downfall of Rico and the terrible
revenge of the horse . . . with great relish and giggling, you
describe Rico's plight. You hate Rico so, that for a moment
you are the horse."[4]

Fearful for St. Mawr's fate, Rachel and Lou spirit him
away to America, accompanied by the grooms, Lewis and

[Facing page] Fig. 19. Arroyo Seco cave in winter. Described by
Lawrence in the last scene of "The Woman Who Rode Away."
Photograph by James Buechler, courtesy of the photographer.

Phoenix, later to leave them in Texas and move on to New Mexico. Lou procures a ranch in the wilderness of New Mexico's mountains and retreats into a lone existence, "something bigger than men, bigger than people, bigger than religion. It is something to do with wild America. . . . Now I know where I want to be, with the wild spirit that wants me."[5]

As noted earlier, the ranch that Lou bought was named "Las Chivas," Spanish for "female goats." The second owners of what became the Kiowa Ranch, the McClures, raised Angora goats.

The theme of mastery versus submission is clear in these tales. The last line of "The Woman Who Rode Away" reads, "The mastery that man must hold, and that passes from race to race." The critic Herbert Meredith Orrell observes, "At the very root of all of Lawrence's writings is the view of the creation as dualistic—male opposing female, light opposing darkness, flesh opposing spirit, creation opposing destruction."[6]

Sitting outside the cabin one morning, Lawrence coughed up blood; Frieda was terrified. Lawrence stayed in bed until the following day. He was enraged to learn that Frieda had sent for the local physician, "Doc" Martin, from Taos. Lawrence screamed at her that he hated doctors, but Frieda insisted that the doctor could only be of help. When the doctor told him it was just bronchial trouble that could be eased with a mustard poultice, Lawrence was relieved.

Another account of the event suggests that "Doc" Martin wanted to take Lawrence back to Taos for treatment, but Frieda insisted on treating him herself.

At another time, one evening at the ranch, Lawrence coughed up blood while he was reading sections of *St. Mawr* to Frieda and Brett. He was clearly not well.

Later that summer, Mabel took the Lawrences and Brett to Arizona to witness the Hopi Snake Dance. Lawrence felt his usual disdain for the dance and the people who came to watch it:

The south-west is the great playground of the white American. The desert isn't good for anything else. And the Indian, with his long hair and bits of pottery and clumsy home-made trinkets, he's a wonderful toy to play with.[7]

Nevertheless, when it came time to write an article on the Hopi Snake Dance for *The Adelphi* magazine, Lawrence took a more serious tone, exploring the religious aspects more and eliminating the derision:

> Amid all its crudity and the sensationalism which comes chiefly out of the crowd's desire for thrills, one cannot help pausing in reverence before the delicate, anointed bravery of the snake-priests.[8]

Although relationships between Lawrence and Mabel had once again taken a turn for the worse (someone had told her that Lawrence called her "dangerous and destructive"), on October 8, 1924, Mabel drove the Lawrences and Brett to Santa Fe, where they headed for Mexico—ultimately, to Oaxaca.

MEXICO AND OAXACA

In Oaxaca, Brett and the Lawrences stayed at the Hotel Francia. A week or so later, the Lawrences rented a house, which came with two green parrots and a fat dog named "Corasmin." This group formed the basis for one of

Lawrence's most charming essays, "Corasmin and the Parrots," the first part of *Mornings in Mexico*. The travel essays in the book had all appeared in magazines such as *The Adelphi*, *Laughing Horse*, and *Theatre Arts Monthly*. The essays are divided between accounts of Old Mexico and the American Southwest. Assembled as a book, it was dedicated by Lawrence to "Mabel Lujan" [*sic*].

Lawrence fell ill in Oaxaca, having contracted malaria. After consultations with local physicians, Frieda took him to Mexico City, where a Dr. Uhfelder conducted a thorough examination, including blood tests, then told Frieda that Lawrence had tuberculosis. He advised Frieda that Lawrence had only a year or two to live, that a sea voyage or the cold climate of England would be harmful, and that a warmer climate—in Mexico or back at the ranch in Taos—was critical for his health. After a couple of days in El Paso, where he was detained by immigration officials, partly because of his unhealthy state, Lawrence, with help from American and British diplomatic officials and a bit of rouge to liven up his cheeks, got across the border. ∽

CHAPTER FIVE

Taos III

April to September 1925

The first week of April 1925, Andrew Dasburg, a Taos artist whom Mabel had lured to Taos, met the Lawrences in Santa Fe and drove them to the Kiowa Ranch. Brett had gone before and was staying at a cabin on the Hawks' ranch. Lawrence was still weak, and the chores he would have liked to perform were done instead by his Taos Indian friend Trinidad, and Trinidad's wife, Rufina.

Mabel was in Taos the summer of 1925, but she and Lawrence did not meet, apparently owing to people gossiping on the one hand to him, saying that she considered the Lawrences to have sponged upon her, and on the other hand to Mabel, saying that Lawrence had made negative comments about her. Indeed, they never saw each other again. Although there was obvious tension between them, there remained a mutual respect that transcended the petty disputes, and when Mabel completed the first volume of her four-volume autobiography, she sent the manuscript to Lawrence in Italy for his criticism. They corresponded until his death in 1930.

Lawrence was improving in his health enough that by May he was once again working on revising his novel *Quetzalcoatl*, based in Mexico. This was the title Lawrence had chosen for his novel about ancient religion and the legendary Aztec god Quetzalcoatl, whose name meant "feathered serpent." The publishers, Lawrence wrote to a friend, "went into a panic" and wanted to call it *The Plumed Serpent*.

Lawrence was determined to return to Europe. It was also true that their six-month visa was soon to expire. On August 28, 1925, he wrote to a friend:

> We leave here Sept. 10th—expect to be in England by first week in October. . . . I am quite well. It grieves me to leave my horses, and my cow Susan, and the cat Timsy Wemyss, and the white cock Moses, and the place.[1]

As an aside, names for the Lawrence animals such as "Moses" and "Susan" are commonplace, but the question of so unusual a name as "Timsy Wemyss" is a tantalizing one, fortunately answered by Diana Trilling, who in a footnote to her edited Lawrence letters notes that Lady Cynthia Asquith, a friend of Lawrence, was the daughter of the 11th Earl of Wemyss.[2]

On September 11, Lawrence's fortieth birthday, Bill Hawk drove the Lawrences down from the mountain, eventually via Denver and New York, to board the SS *Resolute* for England. From England, they went to Germany and ended their trip in Italy. He never forgot the ranch. On November 25, 1925, Lawrence was by the seaside in Spotorno, Italy, writing his essay "A Little Moonshine with Lemon" for the special Lawrence issue of *Laughing Horse*.[3]

Brett had remained in New Mexico, and on December 12, 1929, Lawrence wrote her from the Villa Beau Soleil in Bandol, France:

I really think I shall try to come back in the spring. I begin to believe I shall never get well over here. My health is no better this year than last—it's

really worse—and I hardly walk a stride. . . . How
I hate it. Perhaps if I came back to New Mexico I
would get up again.[4]

Lawrence never did return to New Mexico. He died in
Vence, France, on March 2, 1930.

LAWRENCE, TENNESSEE WILLIAMS, AND TAOS

In 1959 Tennessee Williams, an admirer of Lawrence,
produced *I Rise in Flame, Cried the Phoenix*, portraying
Lawrence's death in France. He captured Lawrence's
expressed desire to return to New Mexico: "Now I want to
get back to the desert and try all over again to become a
savage."[5] Williams also creates a mood of love and struggle
between Frieda and Lawrence. In his scene where Lawrence
is dying, Williams has Lawrence plead with Frieda:

I have a nightmarish feeling that while I'm dying,
I'll be surrounded by women.—They'll burst in
the door and the windows the moment I lose the
strength to push them away—they'll moan and
they'll flutter like doves around the burnt-out

Phoenix.—They'll cover my face and my hands
with flimsy kisses and little trickling tears . . .
don't want that. I want to die like a lonely old
animal does.[6]

Williams had written to his agent, Audrey Wood, in
October 1941 that he was writing

a play about D. H. Lawrence which absorbs me
more at the moment because of my long and
deep interest in his work and ideas . . . Lawrence
was a funny little man, a sort of furious bantam
surrounded by large and impressionable hens—
excluding Frieda who is truly magnificent.[7]

Williams's play was not produced until 1959 in the off-
Broadway Theatre de Lys for just one performance. The
reviewer in the *Saturday Review* of April 28, 1959, called
it "Tennessee Williams' purest piece of dramatic writing."
He goes on to say, "Indeed it is so pure that the playwright,
when he wrote it in 1949, did not believe it could be
performed in the theatre."

Williams had been interested in Lawrence for many years before he wrote the play. He had written a letter to Frieda on July 29, 1939:

> Dear Mrs. Lawrence:
>
> Writing this letter is rather insane as I have no idea as to your exact address. I am only vaguely persuaded that you are still living in New Mexico, in the vicinity of Taos. Briefly, I am a young writer who has a profound admiration for your late husband's work and had conceived the idea, perhaps fantastic, of writing a play about him, dramatizing not so much his life as his ideas or philosophy which strike me as being the richest expressed in modern writing. I have read your deeply moving biography, *Not I, But The Wind* and am convinced that you would be entirely sympathetic toward any work undertaken to advance the world's knowledge and appreciation of your husband's genius.[8]

In the fall of 1939, Williams visited Taos. He was still known as "Tom," having been born Thomas Lanier Williams III. He had an appointment with one of the prominent merchants in Taos, Albert Gusdorf, who owned a department store on the plaza. Williams's father, Cornelius Coffin Williams, known as "C. C.," was manager of the International Shoe Company in St. Louis; Gusdorf's store carried their brand, Red Goose Shoes. "C. C." had arranged the meeting between Tom and Gusdorf. Albert was the nephew of Alexander Gusdorf, the original owner of the store. A letter from the auditor of International Shoe Co., dated October 28, 1944, was addressed to Mrs. Albert Gusdorf, referring to a matter of insurance. The Gusdorfs were also important figures in Taos's cultural life. As Lyle Leverich notes, Gusdorf's wife and daughter were in charge of the Harwood library and museum.[9] Tom wrote to his mother in August 1939 that "the museum was Mrs. Gusdorf's old family home—she is a descendant of Spanish first settlers and very proud and aristocratic. In the library they have everything written by or about Lawrence!" Mrs. Gusdorf was born Margarita Simpson ("Maggie") to Henry Smith Simpson, an officer in St. Vrain's regiment and Kit Carson's as well. Simpson had married Maria Josefa Valdez around 1868. She was the daughter of Juan de Jesus and Maria Juliana Valdez, whose home later was the home of the Harwoods, now the Southwest Research Center and Harwood Museum of the University of New Mexico.

It was not only the Gusdorfs who welcomed Williams. He was given a warm reception by Dorothy Brett, to whom he was introduced by Mrs. Gusdorf. Brett organized social events for him; Frieda also entertained him and was so taken by Tom that she actually offered him a piece of land on the Kiowa Ranch to build on. He turned down this generous offer and moved on, heading back east. He said that after three days in the cabin, Lawrence's ghost proved too overpowering.[10]

Tennessee Williams returned to Taos in 1946 and became violently ill. Rushed to Holy Cross Hospital, managed by nuns, he was operated upon by what he described as "two handsome young doctors." These were the physicians Albert Rosen and Ashley Pond. Accounts of this surgery, usually described in writings about Williams, refer to it as an appendectomy, but it was not. Williams

himself calls it an operation for *"Maecles Diverticulum."*
The medical problem is now called Meckel's diverticulum,
named after the German comparative anatomist Johann
Meckel, whose Latin name was Maecles. The problem, a
rare genetic disease, involved an inflamed intestinal pouch
that required removal.

A few days after surgery, Williams called Frieda, who
picked him up at the hospital and took him up to the
ranch. On the way, Tennessee wrote, they "stopped at a
cantina along the road and purchased a big jug of wine
and we drank and laughed as we went up the mountain
and then all at once I found myself breathless."[11] The
alcohol, combined with the altitude (Taos at 7,000 feet,
San Cristobal at 8,500 feet) so soon after surgery, took its
toll, and Williams was rushed back to the hospital. About
this time, Frieda wrote to Una Jeffers, the wife of poet
Robinson Jeffers, that she really liked Tennessee. ∾

CHAPTER SIX

The D. H. Lawrence "Forbidden Paintings"

When Lawrence died, he left no will, and legal battles over his estate ensued between Frieda and members of his family—particularly his brother George, whom Lawrence had not even seen during the latter part of his life. Frieda was successful in gaining her share and control of his manuscripts. Upon Frieda's death, Angelo, as Frieda's surviving husband, inherited her estate. He remarked to his friend Saki Karavas, the owner of the Hotel La Fonda on Taos Plaza: "Poor Lawrence. He never knew who he was working for!"[1] Angelo sold the paintings to Saki, who hung them in the Hotel La Fonda and named them "D. H. Lawrence's Forbidden Paintings" because they had been seized by the police as obscene in Dorothy Warren's gallery in London in 1929. While none of the paintings were created in Taos, they have become a popular attraction for visitors interested in Lawrence, who come to Taos to visit the ranch and see his art. Now restored by the current owner of the Hotel La Fonda, the Sahd family, they hang in a special, well-lighted room off the hotel lobby. There is a small fee charged for viewing the paintings.

Lawrence was interested in art from an early age. By the age of seventeen, he was an accomplished copier of art, and from 1908 to 1911, in his role as a teacher at Croydon's Davidson Road School, he taught art and nature study and encouraged his young students to take an interest in drawing. He pursued his interest in art while touring Europe, and became familiar with artists from the Italian Renaissance to French modernism—such as Cézanne, whom he greatly admired. Primitive and Futurist art fascinated him.

He continued his interest in art. In 1924, when in Taos at the ranch, Lawrence observed Brett painting the Kiowa Ranch landscape. Brett writes that Lawrence said, "Here move away," and that he shoved her aside. Lawrence went on to say, "If that is Susan [his cow] Lord help her. She'll never stand on her legs like that, let alone run as you have made her." And Brett comments, "With careful fingers you make a wild, fleeing Susan." Further on, Brett writes that Lawrence said, "I'll put Timsy [his cat] just here," and that Lawrence painted Timsy arching her back.[2] The painting, *Kiowa Ranch* by Dorothy Brett, now resides in the Casa Benavides in Taos, owned by the McCarthys, who inherited it from Saki Karavas.

Lawrence was not shy about shoving an artist aside, as Brett said he did to her while painting. Knud Merrild, one of the two Danish painters who lived next to the Lawrences on the Del Monte Ranch in the winter of 1923, recounts, in his *A Poet and Two Painters*, Lawrence's strong interest in watching him paint, and reports that on one occasion, Lawrence tried to grab the brush out of his hand in order to paint part of the picture himself.[3] Merrild had to struggle with Lawrence in order to retrieve the brush; Brett was much more patient. Joseph Foster, a young writer who wrote a very personal, almost adulatory book about Lawrence in Taos, commented that Knud Merrild and Kai Götzche were "second-rate artists,"[4] a judgment apparently not shared by the Los Angeles Museum of Art, which mounted a major exhibition of Merrild's work in 1965. Foster had an interesting view of artists. Writing of Walter Ufer, a friend and admirer of Lawrence and a member of the Taos Society of Artists, Foster says, "Ufer was an abandoned, lonely, inarticulate man, as all artists must of necessity be."[5]

It was not until 1926, the year after he and Frieda had departed from Taos for the last time, that Lawrence seriously began to take up painting. The occasion was a gift by Maria Huxley, Aldous's Belgian wife. She brought over to the Villa Mirenda in Florence, where the Lawrences were living, a gift of four canvases that had been left in the villa where the Huxleys were staying. Lawrence's response: "I sat on the floor with the canvases propped against a chair—and with my house-paint brushes and colours in little casseroles, I disappeared into that canvas."[6]

Barbara Weekley Barr, Frieda's daughter, encouraged Lawrence in his painting. She writes in a memoir that Lawrence was very pleased with his paintings, which took less toll on him than writing. He said he was going to give up being an author and paint instead.[7] It is to our good fortune that he did not.

Barbara was a trained artist in her own right, having studied at the prestigious London Slade School of Fine Arts (as had Brett and Taos's Blanche Grant), and she had spoken with Dorothy Warren, who owned a gallery in London, about mounting a show of Lawrence's paintings. Warren agreed, and on June 14, 1929, the show opened with twenty-five of his works. The climate for the show was somewhat uneasy in view of the negative publicity that had surrounded the release, the previous year, of his book *Lady Chatterley's Lover*, which spoke out for sexual freedom (and perhaps more importantly, for relations between members of different classes of society). The book had been suppressed as obscene by the authorities, just as his work *The Rainbow* had been seized by the authorities and banned in 1915. Lawrence's reputation was that of an iconoclast, an outspoken advocate of sexual freedom, and a social rebel. This reputation, in all probability, led to a record crowd of some 13,000 people paying a shilling each to view the exhibition. Some of the visitors complained to the police about what they considered to be the obscene nature of the artworks, and acting upon orders from the home secretary, six policemen entered the Dorothy Warren Gallery and seized thirteen of the paintings, along with books, the Mandrake editions of the paintings. On August 8, 1929, at the Marlborough Street Police Court, the decision to ban the paintings was officially made.

The main criterion for seizing the works appears to be the portrayal of pubic hair. After a threat to burn the paintings and ensuing legal action, the paintings were restored to Dorothy Warren with the proviso that they not be put on public display. Lawrence had received word of the legal actions while he was living in Italy, and was much distressed by the events. He instructed Warren to compromise with the authorities rather than risk the destruction of the works. Warren also finalized the agreement that they would never again be shown on British soil, an injunction that apparently still stands in the United Kingdom.

The paintings were released and, in 1930, were taken to Vence, France, where they were kept at Martha Gordon Crotch's pottery shop. The paintings were scattered, some bought by collectors, some given away to friends of the Lawrences. When Frieda returned to New Mexico with Ravagli, she had in her possession ten of the original set of twenty-five, and these constitute the La Fonda collection.

SAKI KARAVAS AND THE PAINTINGS

Saki Karavas, now the owner of the Lawrence paintings, was of Greek heritage and fiercely interested in and proud of Greek culture. He was also something of a playful imp. In figure 20, behind the wreath of cigar smoke, one can see some of Lawrence's paintings. Half seriously, he carried on a long-standing correspondence with British officials in which he offered to send the D. H. Lawrence paintings, which he now owned, back to the United Kingdom if they, in turn, would return "the Marbles" to Greece. The Elgin Marbles, consisting of a fifth-century B.C. frieze and sculpture torn from the Parthenon and other buildings on the Acropolis, were taken by Thomas Bruce, the 7th Earl of Elgin, to London in 1806 and placed in the British Museum, where they still reside. Lord Elgin was the British ambassador to Constantinople (1799–1803) and received permission from the Ottoman sultan Selim III to remove the treasures to England. Saki wrote numerous letters, one in 1976 to the British home secretary offering the trade. A typical exchange occurred in late 1989 and early 1990, when Saki wrote a letter to "The Rt. Hon. Neil G. Kinnock, M.P." that began:

I believe I am correct in recalling you made a statement some years ago that you would act to restore the Elgin Marbles to Greece in the likely event that a Parliamentary majority of your party raised you to first lord of the treasury and prime minister. My recollection was that Melina Mercouri [famous Greek actress and Minister of Culture for Greece] was in London at the time seeking support for the Marbles.

The purpose of my letter is to suggest that in the likely event you become Head of H.M. Government and indeed move to return the Marbles, I would like to show my gratitude by returning to Great Britain the important paintings, ten in all, by D. H. Lawrence, which are now in my possession.[8]

Saki's letter continued to review a bit of the history of the paintings. A letter, dated February 5, 1990, was sent to Saki in reply. The stationery was that of "The Office of the Leader of the Opposition, House of Commons" and was signed by "Charles Clarke, Personal Assistant to Neil Kinnock." It read:

Fig. 20. Saki Karavas. Reproduced by permission of the photographer, Paul O'Connor.

> Mr. Kinnock's views on the Elgin Marbles are well
> known, and he does not regard these matters as
> appropriate for "quid pro quo" bargains. Obviously
> the return of D. H. Lawrence's paintings to Britain
> would be worthwhile.[9]

Saki never failed to pursue the exchange, though fruitless, and thoroughly enjoyed his interactions with the stalwarts of H.M. government, as well as the many newspaper and magazine articles his publicity regarding the Lawrence paintings generated. Recent events revived the memory of Saki's efforts to retrieve the Elgin Marbles when the Greek government, through the office of the mayor of Athens, requested their return at the start of the 2004 Summer Olympics in Athens. Greece received the same response of refusal Saki had encountered years back.

The paintings were recently restored by the present owners. It appears that this is the first time they have been restored since the time when Frieda asked her young friend, artist Earl Stroh, to help with a restoration. Earl, now an internationally renowned artist recently deceased, was a close friend of Frieda and Angelo. In his book, *Journey with Genius*,[10] Witter Bynner writes of an evening in his home in Santa Fe, when Frieda read from the galleys of her forthcoming book, *Not I, But the Wind*, in which her glasses clouded from the emotion of reading about Lawrence. Although not at this evening event, Earl frequently joined Frieda in visits to friends such as Bynner.

Earl described his role in the paintings' restoration in an interview with Michael Squires and Lynn Talbot, published in their book *Living at the Edge*:

Frieda once said to me, "I've got all those paintings of Lawrence's and they're beginning to fall apart. Do you think you could save them?" I said, "Well, I could do my best." And I'm afraid I did. Do you know what they're painted on? Old fashioned window shades that you pull down. They were cheesecloth impregnated with God knows what! That's what they were painted on, and they were painted with little cans of cheap enamel out of a five-and-ten-cent store.... Being on that self-destructing, highly acidic stuff, they were getting brittle. So I mounted them on . . . Masonite![11]

Stroh's comment about restoring the paintings—"And I'm afraid I did"—reveals an artist's critical eye as to the paintings' merit. Others have said that the paintings reflect the passion and abandon with which Lawrence wrote. Whatever the artistic merit, the paintings form a valuable insight into Lawrence's life.

End of an Era

After Lawrence's death, Frieda remained in Taos, buying a home near the Mesa and a winter retreat for herself and Angelo near Port Isabel, Texas—close to Brownsville. In one trip to Texas in 1949, Frieda was interviewed by a reporter from a Texas newspaper who asked what her favorite D. H. Lawrence work was. After a moment's thought, Frieda replied:

> *Twilight in Italy*. We had such a wonderful time on those trips in Italy and he wrote about them so beautifully. Yes, that is my favorite I believe.[12]

Frieda died on her seventy-seventh birthday—August 11, 1956—and is buried next to the memorial on the ranch. Figure 21 shows what is believed to be the last photograph of Frieda, by Regina Cooke. The ranch was deeded in her will to the University of New Mexico. The will, filed and dated August 23, 1956, was signed by "Frieda Emma Johanna Maria Lawrence Ravagli"—all of her names except Von Richthofen.

Fig. 21. Frieda Lawrence, probably last photograph taken of her. Photograph by Regina Cooke. Author's collection.

"THE BRETT"

Dorothy Brett, who had carved an important niche for herself as an artist, also remained in Taos. There are still many residents of Taos who knew her well, respected and loved her. Genevieve Jansen was cofounder with Claire Morrill of the Taos Bookshop in 1947, now sadly out of business. Genevieve recounted an anecdote in which she, Brett, and Claire were invited to attend a Hopi ceremony on Second Mesa by a friend, Helen Blumenschein.[13] Helen was the daughter of the Taos Society of Artists' Ernest Blumenschein and Mary Green Blumenschein, a fine artist in her own right. Helen was also an artist and a writer, and in addition, she was passionate about archaeology and was working on the Hopis' Second Mesa in Arizona. Brett was not able to attend, but Genevieve and Claire went to the Hopi Reservation to take part. The ceremony was held in a kiva, an underground room used for religious purposes, although in view of the invitation to outsiders, this particular ceremony was not sacred. Genevieve told of climbing down the wooden ladder to enter the kiva. With the smoke, the closed and almost airless space, and the crowd, Genevieve soon felt herself becoming ill.

She pushed through the crowd to reach the ladder and climbed, escaping to the night air. A few days after they returned to Taos, Genevieve received a telephone call from Brett, who asked how the trip had gone. Genevieve told her about the whole embarrassing event and how she had disgraced herself by becoming ill and pushing her way to escape. Brett listened, and told Genevieve that she knew how Genevieve must have felt. "Why," she said, "the exact same thing happened to me in the Houses of Parliament!" Brett died in Taos on August 27, 1977, at the age of ninety-three.

LAWRENCE'S ASHES

Lawrence never returned to New Mexico. On March 2, 1930, he died in the Villa Aurella, in the hill town of Vence in France. In 1935 his ashes were brought to Taos by Frieda's lover, Angelo Ravagli, whom she eventually married in 1950. According to a story in the *Taos Valley News* of May 2, 1935, "Captain Angelo Ravagli, when he arrived in Taos last week from Europe, brought with him the ashes of the late D. H. Lawrence . . ." And there was to be a "simple burial ceremony . . . in the near future according to Mrs. Lawrence."[14] The ashes were finally interred on September 19, 1935.

There are many legends surrounding Lawrence's ashes. What seems true is that Mabel wanted to scatter the ashes around the Sangre de Cristo mountains to which Lawrence was devoted. In this plan, she apparently had the aid of Brett, but Frieda wanted them installed in the memorial that Angelo had built at the ranch. One story, much credited, has it that Frieda and Angelo forgot the ashes on the platform of the railroad station at Lamy and had to drive back to retrieve them. Roy Taylor, a recent owner of the now closed tavern "Legal Tender," situated at the Lamy station since the 1880s, told interviewers that the ashes were in an urn, which had been left in the bar and dumped out, to be replaced by wood ash and later retrieved.[15]

Another version of what happened to the ashes when Angelo and Frieda forgot them in Lamy remains the one that is perhaps the most interesting of all. It is recounted by the present owners of the Inn of the Turquoise Bear at Poet's Corner, in Santa Fe. The inn was the home of Witter Bynner, and the owners, Ralph Bolton and Robert Frost, tell the story that when Angelo and Frieda left the urn of ashes at the railroad station in Lamy, they telephoned Witter in Santa Fe and asked him to go to Lamy and retrieve the urn and its precious contents. Rather than return the ashes, it is said, Bynner replaced them with wood ash, and then dipped a teaspoon of them in his tea every morning to partake of the great man's genius.[16] While there is no confirmation of this story, nor many of the others, it reflects the aura Lawrence's ashes have surrounding them.

Eya Fechin, the daughter of the Russian émigré artist Nicolai Fechin, who lived and painted in Taos from 1923 to 1935, once said that Brett swore to her dying day that they had replaced Lawrence's ashes with those of a burned dead dog, scattering the true ashes in the mountains.[17] Another charming tale is told of a fight between Mabel and Frieda over the disposition of the ashes that was witnessed by a friend who, fearing for the ashes' safety, stole them and took them to Alexandra "Tinka" Fechin, the wife of Nicolai Fechin. The story goes that the ashes were placed in the corner of the dining room of the Fechin House, in the iconostasis, the cabinet that held the Russian icons. In

Russia, this sacred location, always in the northeastern corner, is called the "Red Corner" or the "Beautiful Corner." According to a slightly different version told by Eya Fechin, the charming tale of ashes saved from disaster takes on a new twist: the ashes were indeed kept in the Beautiful Corner, but only because Angelo and Frieda had stopped off to see Tinka, had several drinks, left and forgot them once again, only to retrieve them a few days later.[18]

Confirmation of the struggle among Mabel, Frieda, and Brett about the disposition of the ashes comes from another longtime Taos resident, Jane Mingenbach, who recounts a story of the noted artist Gisella Loeffler, once owner with her husband, Frank Chase, of the "Pink House." Gisella dropped by Mabel's house only to enter and find the three women fiercely engaged in a loud verbal fight over the ashes. Gisella wisely withdrew.[19]

The ashes were placed in the ranch memorial on September 15, 1935, at a ceremony reported in the local newspaper, the *Taos Valley News*, a copy of which Mary Wheeler, a longtime resident of Taos, shared with the author. She was a young girl when she attended

the ceremony. Stewart Barr (the husband of Barbara
Weekley Barr, Frieda's daughter) read the eulogy, a part
of which read:

What a troublous life he had—a life of conflict.
That was inevitable in a man whose whole being
revolted against stagnation, hypocrisy, and the
deadening limitations of the culture of his time.[20]

In a fit of pique, it has been suggested, Mabel Luhan
told Tony to pass the word along to the Taos Pueblo that
they were not to take part in the ceremony. Tony did spread
the word among the Taos Pueblo Indians that they should
never disturb the grave of a great man or they and their
families would be forever cursed. And they were not to
participate in the ceremony to inter Lawrence's ashes—a
bit more intrigue surrounding the event. Then we find a
story published in *John O'London's Weekly* with an account
of the ceremony at the ranch by a reporter who writes that
Frieda was forced to bring in Indians "from a distance."[21]
This account is readily refuted by the newspaper story in
the September 19, 1935, issue of the *Taos Valley News*:

> Four Indians, Trinidad Archuleta and Adam
> and Cruz Trujillo from Taos Pueblo and Canuto
> Suazo from Tesuque [a Pueblo near Santa Fe]
> sang several Indian funeral songs to the soft beat
> of their drums, then danced briefly.[22]

Any injunction by Mabel against participation by the Taos
Pueblo was obviously ignored. Trinidad's devotion to
Lawrence shows in this event, as well as in the painting of
the buffalo Trinidad did in 1934 on the side of Lawrence's
cabin on the ranch, four years after Lawrence's death and
one year before the interment of the ashes.

Barbara Barr writes in her memoirs of Lawrence
that Frieda had arranged for a local judge to read the
oration, but that someone had "tampered" with him and
so Barbara's husband, Stewart, filled in.[23] More intrigue.
Mabel apparently was up to her old tricks, acting, as Jake
Page described her in the *Smithsonian Magazine*, like "a
charged particle among the force fields of her time."[24]

As recorded in the newspaper story, a Taoseña,
Mrs. Merriam Golden, read one of Lawrence's last poems
as a prayer:

Give me the moon at my feet.
Set my feet upon the crescent like a Lord,
O let my ankles be bathed in moonlight,
That I may go sure and moon-shod,
Cool and bright-footed toward my goal.[25]

∾

APPENDIX A

Works Written by D. H. Lawrence during His Stays in Taos*

1922

September

Wrote essay, "Indians and an Englishman," following a trip to Jicarilla Apache Reservation

Wrote essay, "Taos," describing the Taos Pueblo San Geronimo Festival

Wrote first paragraphs of essay, "Certain Americans and an Englishman," attacking Bursum Bill

October

Revised novel of Australia, *Kangaroo*

Five poems for *Birds, Beasts and Flowers*: "Autumn in Taos," "Eagle in New Mexico," "Men in New Mexico," "The Red Wolf," and "Spirits Summoned West"

November

Rewrote work of criticism, *Studies in Classic American Literature*

---

* Drawn from Sagar's comprehensive listing and discussion of Lawrence's writings: Keith Sagar, *D. H. Lawrence: A Calendar of His Works*, with a checklist of the manuscripts of D. H. Lawrence by Lindeth Vasey (Austin: University of Texas Press, 1979).

December

Finished *Studies in Classic American Literature*

Probably wrote poem "Blue Jay"

1923

January

Revised *Little Novels of Sicily*

Wrote poem, "Bibbles," about his dog "Pips"

Wrote poem "Mountain Lion"

February

Wrote essays "Surgery for the Novel or a Bomb" and "Model
   Americans"

Finished *Birds, Beasts and Flowers*

March

Wrote poem "American Eagle"

Lawrence was traveling away from New Mexico from March
   1923 to April 1924, after which he returned to Taos. He had
   traveled to Mexico, England, and France, with trips to Los
   Angeles, New York, and Buffalo in the interim.

1924

April

Wrote essays "The Dance of the Sprouting Corn" and "O,
   Americans!"

Wrote the sketch of a play, *David*, for actress Ida Rauh

May
Wrote essay "Pan in America"

June
Finished "Pan in America"
Wrote novelette "The Woman Who Rode Away"
Began play *Altitude* (never completed)
Began novelette *St. Mawr*

August
Wrote "The Hopi Snake Dance" upon return from Hopi
    Reservation
Finished *St. Mawr*

September
Wrote epilogue to *Movements in European History*
Began novelette "The Princess"

October
Finished "The Princess"
(On October 16 Lawrence left for Mexico, and returned to Taos in
    April of 1925.)

1925
May
Finished play *David*

June

Revised Mexican novel "Quetzalcoatl" (later named *The Plumed Serpent*)

Wrote several essays on the novel, including "Art and Morality" and "Why the Novel Matters"

July

Wrote essays comprised in *Reflections on the Death of a Porcupine*

August

Finished *Reflections on the Death of a Porcupine*

Lawrence left the United States for England on September 19, 1925, never to return to Taos.

November

In November 1925, Lawrence was in Spotorno, Italy, where he wrote the essay reminiscing about the "Little Ranch in New Mexico" for Spud Johnson's magazine, *The Laughing Horse*. The essay, "A Little Moonshine with Lemon," was published in the April 1926 issue of the magazine. The title came from a nostalgic wish for the drink, "moonshine" or somewhat illegally brewed whiskey with a bit of lemon, that he had enjoyed on the "Ranch in New Mexico." The occasion was the celebration of St. Catherine's Day in Italy, and the only drink Lawrence could get was wine.

Notes

CHAPTER ONE

1. Frieda Lawrence, quoted in Haruhide Mori, ed., *A Conversation on D. H. Lawrence* (Los Angeles: Friends of the UCLA Library, 1974), 37. Grateful acknowledgment is made to UCLA Library and the Regents of the University of California for permission to use quotations from Haruhide Mori's work.

2. D. H. Lawrence, letter to the Brewsters from Fontana Vecchia, 2 November 1921, in Harry T. Moore, ed., *The Collected Letters of D. H. Lawrence*, vol. 2 (New York: Viking Press, 1962), 669.

3. G. M. Lacy, ed., *D. H. Lawrence: Letters to Thomas and Adele Seltzer* (Santa Barbara, CA: Black Sparrow Press, 1976), 27.

4. Mabel Dodge Luhan, *Lorenzo in Taos* (New York: Alfred A. Knopf, 1932), 45.

CHAPTER TWO

1. Eliot Fay, *Lorenzo in Search of the Sun* (London: Vision Press, 1955).

2. Christopher Lasch, "Mabel Dodge Luhan: Sex as Politics," in *The New Radicalism in America* (New York: Alfred A. Knopf, 1965), 104–40.

3. D. H. Lawrence, "New Mexico," in *Survey Graphic* (East Stroudsburg, PA: Survey Associates, 1928), cited in E. D. McDonald, ed., *Phoenix: The Posthumous Papers of D. H. Lawrence* (New York: Viking Press, 1936), 14.

4. D. H. Lawrence, "Indians and an Englishman," *The Dial* (February 1923): 144–52.

5. D. H. Lawrence, quoted in Luhan, *Lorenzo in Taos*, 54.

6. D. H. Lawrence, "Letter to Mary Cannan, September 27, 1922," in Moore, *Collected Letters*, 719–20.

7. Luhan, *Lorenzo in Taos*, 72.

8. Frieda Lawrence, quoted in Mori, *A Conversation*, 34.

9. Robert Lucas, *Frieda Lawrence: The Story of Frieda von Richthofen and D. H. Lawrence* (New York: Viking Press, 1973), 261.

10. Ibid.

11. Joseph Foster, *D. H. Lawrence in Taos* (Albuquerque: University of New Mexico Press, 1972), 98.

12. D. H. Lawrence, quoted in Luhan, *Lorenzo in Taos*, 106.

13. Letter to D. H. Lawrence, dictated by Tony Luhan to Mabel Dodge Luhan (see fig. 5). Courtesy of Richard W. Godin.

14. Ibid.

15. Keith Sagar, ed., *D. H. Lawrence and New Mexico* (Paris/London: Alyscamps Press, 1995), 23.

16. Eliot Fay, *Lorenzo in Search of the Sun*, 72.

17. Dorothy Brett, *Lawrence and Brett: A Friendship* (Santa Fe, NM: Sunstone Press, 1974), 228–29, with permission from Sunstone Press and Roger Thomas, executor of the John Manchester Estate. First edition was published by J. B. Lippincott in Philadelphia, 1933.

18. Walton Hawk, personal communication with author, 2003.

19. Dorothy Brandenburg, personal communication with author, 2005.

20. Keith Cushman, "Lawrence and Knud Merrild: New Perspectives," in Keith Cushman and Earl Ingersoll, eds., *D. H. Lawrence: New Worlds* (Madison, NJ: Fairleigh Dickinson University Press, 2003), 71.

21. G. M. Lacy, *D. H. Lawrence: Letters*, 124.

CHAPTER THREE

1. Eliot Fay, *Lorenzo in Search of the Sun*, 68.

2. Dorothy Brett, *Lawrence and Brett*, 133.

3. Ibid., 55.

4. D. H. Lawrence, *St. Mawr* (New York: Alfred A. Knopf, 1925).

5. Tina Ferris and Virginia Hyde, "Nomination of the D. H. Lawrence Ranch to the National Register of Historic Places," D. H. Lawrence Society of North America, 20, www.wsu.edu/~hydev/dhl/dhlnsa.htm.

6. John Collier, in Edward Nehls, *D. H. Lawrence: A Composite Biography*, vol. 2, *1919–1925* (Madison: University of Wisconsin Press, 1958), 198.

7. Dorothy Brett, *Lawrence and Brett*, 69–70.

8. Paul Horgan, "1937: Frieda Lawrence and the Tomb," in *Tracings: A Book of Partial Portraits* (New York: Farrar, Giroux, 1993), 81–102.

9. D. H. Lawrence, "A Little Moonshine with Lemon," *Laughing Horse* (Taos, New Mexico), April 1926; reprinted in Keith Sagar, ed., *D. H. Lawrence and New Mexico*, 101.

10. D. H. Lawrence, quoted in G. M. Lacy, *D. H. Lawrence: Letters*, 124.

11. Dorothy Brett, *Lawrence and Brett*, 81.

12. Ibid.

CHAPTER FOUR

1. D. H. Lawrence, letter to Catherine Carswell, 8 October 1924, in A. Huxley, ed., *The Letters of D. H. Lawrence* (London: William Heinemann, Ltd., 1937), 618.

2. James Wood, ed., *Selected Short Stories of D. H. Lawrence* (New York: Modern Library, 1999).

3. D. H. Lawrence, *St. Mawr* (New York: Alfred A. Knopf, 1925), 128.

4. Dorothy Brett, *Lawrence and Brett*, 138.

5. D. H. Lawrence, *St. Mawr*, 221.

6. Herbert Meredith Orrell, "D. H. Lawrence and the Good Society," in *Century*, 6 May 1981, 18.

7. D. H. Lawrence, "Letter to Willard 'Spud' Johnson," August 1924, in Moore, *Collected Letters*, 804.

8. D. H. Lawrence, "The Hopi Snake Dance" (Flagstaff, AZ: Peccary Press, 1980), 20–21.

Chapter Five

1. D. H. Lawrence, "Letter to Mrs. G. R. C. Conway from Del Monte Ranch, Questa," 28 August 1925, in Harry Moore, *Collected Letters*, 849.

2. Diana Trilling, ed., *The Selected Letters of D. H. Lawrence* (New York: Farrar, Straus and Cudahy, 1958), 238.

3. D. H. Lawrence, "A Little Moonshine with Lemon," 101.

4. D. H. Lawrence, letter to Dorothy Brett from Bandol, France, 12 December 1929, in Harry Moore, *Collected Letters*, 1222.

5. Tennessee Williams, excerpt from *I Rise in Flame, Cried the Phoenix*, in *The Theatre of Tennessee Williams*, vol. 7 (New York: New Directions, 1970 and 1981), reprinted by permission of New Directions Publishing Corporation.

6. Ibid.

7. Tennessee Williams, letter to Audrey Wood, 7 October 1941, in A. J. Devlin and N. M. Tischer, eds., *The Selected Letters of Tennessee Williams*, vol. 1, *1920–1924* (New York: New Directions, 2000), 346.

8. Tennessee Williams, letter to Frieda Lawrence, 29 July 1939, in Lyle Leverich, *Tom: The Unknown Tennessee Williams* (New York: Crown Publishers, Inc., 1995), 313–14.

9. Lyle Leverich, *Tom: The Unknown Tennessee Williams*, 313–14.

10. Robert Lucas, *Frieda Lawrence*, 261.

CHAPTER SIX

1. Saki Karavas, personal communication with author, 1989.

2. Dorothy Brett, *Lawrence and Brett*, 253, 255.

3. Knud Merrild, *A Poet and Two Painters: A Memoir of D. H. Lawrence* (New York: Viking Press, 1938).

4. Joseph Foster, *D. H. Lawrence in Taos*, 53.

5. Ibid.

6. D. H. Lawrence, "Making Pictures," in W. Roberts and H. Moore, eds., *Phoenix II: Uncollected, Unpublished, and Other Prose Works by D. H. Lawrence* (New York: Viking Press, 1968), 603.

7. Barbara Weekley Barr, "Memoir of D. H. Lawrence," in Stephen Spender, ed., *D. H. Lawrence: Novelist, Poet, Prophet* (New York: Harper and Row, 1973), 26.

8. Saki Karavas, personal communication with author, 1989.

9. Saki Karavas, personal communication with author, 1989.

10. Witter Bynner, *Journey with Genius: Recollections and Reflections Concerning the D. H. Lawrences* (London: Peter Nevill, 1953), 356.

11. Earl Stroh, "Interview," from Michael Squires and Lynn K. Talbot, *Living at the Edge: A Biography of D. H. Lawrence and Frieda von Richthofen* (Madison: University of Wisconsin Press, 2002), reprinted by permission of the authors, the University of Wisconsin Press, and Earl Stroh.

12. Frieda Lawrence, quoted in Dwight Hunter, "Noted Author's Widow Gives Views on Culture in Texas," *San Angelo (TX) Standard-Times*, November 27, 1949.

13. Genevieve Jansen, personal communication with author, 1997.

14. *Taos Valley News*, May 2, 1935, with permission from *The Taos News*.

15. Roy Taylor, interview in video *Cowboys, Indians, and UFOs* (Sarasota, FL: Destiny Productions, n.d.).

16. Robert Frost and Ralph Bolton, personal communication with author, 2004.

17. Eya Fechin, personal communication with author, 1990.

18. Eya Fechin, personal communication with author, 1990.

19. Jane Mingenbach, personal communication with author, 2003.

20. *Taos Valley News*, September 19, 1935, with permission of *The Taos News*.

21. S. K. Ratcliffe, *John O'London's Weekly*, July 21, 1950.

22. *Taos Valley News*, September 19, 1935.

23. Barr, Barbara Weekley, "Memoir of D. H. Lawrence," 36.

24. Jake Page, "A Charged Particle among the Force-Fields of Her Times," *Smithsonian Magazine*, June 1991, 122–36.

25. "Prayer," *Taos Valley News*, September 19, 1935.

Index